CONTENTS

JUNE 7, 2005

OPENING STATEMENT

WITNESSES

APPENDIX

MATERIAL SUBMITTED FOR THE HEARING RECORD

MUTUAL FUND TRADING ABUSES

HEARING

BEFORE THE

SUBCOMMITTEE ON COMMERCIAL AND ADMINISTRATIVE LAW

OF THE

COMMITTEE ON THE JUDICIARY HOUSE OF REPRESENTATIVES

ONE HUNDRED NINTH CONGRESS

FIRST SESSION

JUNE 7, 2005

Serial No. 109–42

Printed for the use of the Committee on the Judiciary

Available via the World Wide Web: http://www.house.gov/judiciary

U.S. GOVERNMENT PRINTING OFFICE

21–653 PDF WASHINGTON : 2005

For sale by the Superintendent of Documents, U.S. Government Printing Office
Internet: bookstore.gpo.gov Phone: toll free (866) 512–1800; DC area (202) 512–1800
Fax: (202) 512–2250 Mail: Stop SSOP, Washington, DC 20402–0001

COMMITTEE ON THE JUDICIARY

F. JAMES SENSENBRENNER, Jr., Wisconsin, *Chairman*

HENRY J. HYDE, Illinois
HOWARD COBLE, North Carolina
LAMAR SMITH, Texas
ELTON GALLEGLY, California
BOB GOODLATTE, Virginia
STEVE CHABOT, Ohio
DANIEL E. LUNGREN, California
WILLIAM L. JENKINS, Tennessee
CHRIS CANNON, Utah
SPENCER BACHUS, Alabama
BOB INGLIS, South Carolina
JOHN N. HOSTETTLER, Indiana
MARK GREEN, Wisconsin
RIC KELLER, Florida
DARRELL ISSA, California
JEFF FLAKE, Arizona
MIKE PENCE, Indiana
J. RANDY FORBES, Virginia
STEVE KING, Iowa
TOM FEENEY, Florida
TRENT FRANKS, Arizona
LOUIE GOHMERT, Texas

JOHN CONYERS, Jr., Michigan
HOWARD L. BERMAN, California
RICK BOUCHER, Virginia
JERROLD NADLER, New York
ROBERT C. SCOTT, Virginia
MELVIN L. WATT, North Carolina
ZOE LOFGREN, California
SHEILA JACKSON LEE, Texas
MAXINE WATERS, California
MARTIN T. MEEHAN, Massachusetts
WILLIAM D. DELAHUNT, Massachusetts
ROBERT WEXLER, Florida
ANTHONY D. WEINER, New York
ADAM B. SCHIFF, California
LINDA T. SÁNCHEZ, California
ADAM SMITH, Washington
CHRIS VAN HOLLEN, Maryland

Philip G. Kiko, *General Counsel-Chief of Staff*
Perry H. Apelbaum, *Minority Chief Counsel*

Subcommittee on Commercial and Administrative Law

CHRIS CANNON, Utah *Chairman*

HOWARD COBLE, North Carolina
TRENT FRANKS, Arizona
STEVE CHABOT, Ohio
MARK GREEN, Wisconsin
RANDY J. FORBES, Virginia
LOUIE GOHMERT, Texas

MELVIN L. WATT, North Carolina
WILLIAM D. DELAHUNT, Massachusetts
ADAM SMITH, Washington
CHRIS VAN HOLLEN, Maryland
JERROLD NADLER, New York

Raymond V. Smietanka, *Chief Counsel*
Susan A. Jensen, *Counsel*
James Daley, *Full Committee Counsel*
Stephanie Moore, *Minority Counsel*

MUTUAL FUND TRADING ABUSES

TUESDAY, JUNE 7, 2005

HOUSE OF REPRESENTATIVES,
SUBCOMMITTEE ON COMMERCIAL
AND ADMINISTRATIVE LAW,
COMMITTEE ON THE JUDICIARY,
Washington, DC.

The Subcommittee met, pursuant to notice, at 4:05 p.m., in Room 2141, Rayburn House Office Building, the Honorable Chris Cannon (Chair of the Subcommittee) presiding.

Mr. CANNON. The Committee will come to order. Before I begin my formal remarks, I'd like to welcome the gentlelady from the State of Florida, Ms. Wasserman Schultz, who we anticipate will be named to replace the gentleman from Washington, Mr. Smith, on the Committee. I understand there is a unanimous request that Ms. Wasserman Schultz participate in today's hearing.

Mr. WATT. I ask unanimous consent that Ms. Wasserman Schultz be allowed to participate fully as if she were already a Member of this Committee.

Mr. CANNON. And it has been the habit of this Committee to yield time to a Member of the Committee and have that Member then yield to a person who may be a Member of the full Committee, but not a Member of the Subcommittee. Since Ms. Wasserman Schultz is going to, we hope, become a Member of the Committee quite soon, we will set that precedent aside, and without objection, so ordered. Welcome to the Subcommittee, Ms. Wasserman Schultz.

And now for my formal remarks. In the fall of 2003, the New York State Attorney announced what would become the first of many law enforcement initiatives that his office and other State officials and the SEC would later champion to ferret out mutual fund trading abuses. Within the ensuing months many well-respected mutual fund companies and others were caught up in this scandal, including Canary Capital, Janus Capital Group, Bank of America, Alliance Capital Management, Prudential Securities, Millennium Partners, Fred Alger Management, Putnam Investments, Massachusetts Financial Services, Security Trust, Franklin Resources and Invesco Funds Group.

In the fall and winter of 2003, it seemed as if every day the press reported on yet another shocking instance of mutual fund trading abuses. These abuses included the illegal practice of late trading, which involves trading shares after the markets have closed so that the trader can take advantage of information that becomes available after the closing. The Congressional Research Service analogized this practice to a race track that allows certain customers to bet on yesterday's races.

Other abuses included the more nuanced problem of market timing. Market timing typically involves frequent buying and selling of mutual fund shares by sophisticated investors, such as hedge funds, that seek opportunities to make profits on the differences between foreign and domestic markets.

While not per se illegal, market timing can constitute illegal conduct, if, for example, it takes place as a result of undisclosed agreements between investment advisers and favored customers in contravention of stated fund trading limits. Frequent trading can harm mutual fund shareholders because it lowers fund returns and increases transaction costs.

According to an estimate provided by one of the witnesses at today's hearing, Professor Zitzewitz, market timing abuses may have resulted in $5 billion in annual losses. As of November 2003, the SEC estimated that 50 percent of the 80 largest mutual fund companies had entered into undisclosed arrangements permitting certain shareholders to engage in market timing practices that were inconsistent with the funds' policies, prospectus disclosures or fiduciary obligations.

As the mutual fund scandal unfolded, questions were raised about the fitness of the SEC's overall regulation, inspection, and enforcement of this industry. The Congressional Research Service posed possible explanations, including the following: the possibility that the SEC's resources devoted to the fund industry were dwarfed by the expansion in the number of mutual funds; the possibility that the SEC's overall effectiveness may have been marred by interdivisional disharmonies; the possibility that the SEC officials may have placed too much trust in the fund industry's integrity and ability to police itself; the possibility that the mutual fund industry may be too close to the relevant parts of the SEC entrusted with its oversight and regulation; and the possibility that the SEC may have had a somewhat understandable focus on the prevention of more traditional types of fund misconduct.

In response to these concerns, House Judiciary Committee Chairman Sensenbrenner and Ranking Member Conyers requested the GAO to undertake a comprehensive review of the SEC's efforts to proactively detect and prevent illegal activities in the mutual fund industry. Today's hearing provides an opportunity for GAO to report on its findings and recommendations and to allow the SEC and others to respond to them.

Accordingly, our first witness is Richard Hillman, who is the Director of GAO's Financial Markets and Community Investment Team. With 29 years of experience at GAO, Mr. Hillman is currently responsible for directing research engagements on various cross-cutting financial services matters within the banking securities and insurance industry. Mr. Hillman graduated with honors from the University of Scranton with a bachelor's degree in science and accounting, and has completed additional course work in Government management and information technology issues at the Federal Executive Institute and Harvard's John F. Kennedy School of Government.

Our next witness is Lori Richards, who is the Director of the SEC's Office of Compliance Inspections and Examinations. She has served in that capacity for 10 years. Her office is responsible for administering the SEC's security compliance examination and inspection program for entities registered with the SEC as self-regulatory organizations, broker-dealers, transfer agents, clearing agencies, investment companies and investment advisors. Before beginning her career with the SEC in 1985, Ms. Richards received her B.A. From Northern Illinois University and her J.D. From American University.

Our third witness is William Francis Galvin, the Secretary of the Commonwealth of the Massachusetts. I understand that my colleague on the other side of the aisle Mr. Delahunt would like to say a few words. The gentleman is recognized.

Mr. DELAHUNT. Thank you, Mr. Chairman. I am really pleased to see my friend, my colleague in State government for many years, Bill Galvin here as a witness. He has an extraordinary record as secretary of state. In Massachusetts the securities industry is under his—I should say it is the office that regulates the securities industry in Massachusetts, and he has earned justifiably a national reputation for aggressively protecting investors and has been successful in recovery of millions of dollars for victims of security fraud.

Bill Galvin was an integral part of the 2003 multistate examination of research analysts' practices on Wall Street, which resulted in a finding of fraud against First Boston and developed into investigations into mutual fund industry practices. So it is a pleasure to have you here, Bill, and I look forward to your testimony.

Mr. CANNON. Thank you, Mr. Delahunt.

We are pleased, Mr. Galvin, to have a person of such a national reputation and one who is—I hope can bring to bear, and I believe will bring to bear—a great deal of information and understanding for us on this Committee. Thank you.

Our final witness is Mr. Eric Zitzewitz. He has been an assistant professor of economics at Stanford Graduate School of Business since 2001, and published extensively on the securities industry as well as on other subject matter dealing with economics. He received his undergraduate degree in economics from Harvard and his Ph.D. In economics from MIT.

I extend to each of you my warm regards and appreciation for your willingness to participate in today's hearing. In light of the fact that your written statements will be included in the record, I request that you limit your oral remarks to 5 minutes. And accordingly, please feel free to summarize the salient points of your testimony.

And you will note that there is a lighting system in front of you. After 4 minutes the light will turn from green to yellow, and then at 5 minutes it will turn to red. It's my habit to tap the gavel, probably the handle or maybe a pen, to just indicate that that's happened. You don't need to cut off at that point. We are not trying to cut you off mid-thought, but just as a matter of comity, because there are several people that will want to ask questions today. I can almost assure you that you will have plenty of time to come back and add to your statements as we give 5 minutes to each of the members of the panel.

After you have presented your remarks, the Subcommittee Members in order of their arrival will be permitted to ask questions for 5 minutes. And again, in the case of the clock, I will tap when we get close to when we hit the red light. You don't have to stop immediately, but just as a matter of comity, we would like to move on.

And pursuant to the directive of the Chairman of the Judiciary Committee, I ask the witnesses to please stand and raise your right hand to take the oath.

[Witnesses sworn.]

Mr. CANNON. The record will reflect that each of the witnesses answered in the affirmative.

You may be seated.

And, Mr. Hillman, if you'd like to proceed, you're recognized for 5 minutes.

Mr. HILLMAN. Thank you very much, Mr. Chairman.

Mr. CANNON. Pardon me, Mr. Hillman. If I could interrupt you, we would love to hear from the Ranking Member and I apologize for not having recognized him a moment ago. If the gentleman would like to speak, he is recognized for 5 minutes.

Mr. WATT. Thank you, Mr. Chairman. I won't take 5 minutes. I just wanted an opportunity to join you in welcoming Ms. Wasserman Schultz to the hearing today and hopefully to the membership on the Committee tomorrow, once that is formalized.

I want to thank the Chairman for convening the hearing to begin the process of reviewing the SEC's failure to detect mutual fund abuses. More than one-half of American households invest in mutual funds. They invest to enhance their futures and their children's futures. These investments should be treated with great care and confidently secured from abuses.

I think we all agree the market should be free from unscrupulous activities of mutual fund companies. Although this Subcommittee is addressing the GAO's recommendations with respect to the SEC's role in detecting the mutual fund abuses that hinder long-term shareholders from proper fund returns, I would like to emphasize the important role the States play and continue to play in the collaborative efforts to detect and deter mutual fund abuse.

Many of the abuses examined by the GAO at the request of Chairman Sensenbrenner and Ranking Member Conyers surfaced due to the diligence of the State Attorney General Eliot Spitzer of New York. So while I think it is important that we determine whether the SEC is broken and, if so, how to fix it, I can't overemphasize the critical role that the States must continue to play in protecting investors, large and small.

Additionally, I have—I don't know whether it's enviable, but I serve on both the Judiciary Committee and the House Financial Services Committee, and those are the Committees that actually share jurisdiction over mutual funds and securities. And so I want to emphasize the important role that the Financial Services Committee also plays over law enforcement in the mutual fund industry. I believe we should focus narrowly on enforcement issues in this Subcommittee and take care to divine precisely what role this Committee can and should take in response to the problems of abuses that have been revealed. So I am particularly interested in hearing the testimony here today, and I welcome the witnesses and yield back.

Mr. DELAHUNT. Would the gentleman yield for a moment?

Mr. WATT. I am happy to yield to my friend from Massachusetts.

Mr. DELAHUNT. Yeah, I just wanted to echo some of the sentiments that you expressed, Mr. Watt, particularly regarding the role of the Judiciary Committee as well as the Financial Services Committee. I know you serve on both. And I want to applaud the Chairman for calling this particular hearing into an issue obviously that has great significance and impact to the lives of millions, tens of millions of Americans. And I would hope that this Subcommittee would even be more aggressive in the future in terms of exercising its oversight responsibilities, particularly as it relates to enforcement not only in this area, but in the entire jurisdiction within the Committee's purview.

One can only reflect on the number of administrative bodies that exist in the executive branch of Government that I would respectfully suggest are not the subjects of significant oversight. One only has to think of the alphabet that we deal with in terms of administrative agencies, and yet I have served on this Committee in the past, and this is the first time, in my memory, I can think of a significant agency such as the SEC that has been before the Committee. And I would hope that we would continue to be aggressive and send that message out to the executive branch that this Subcommittee in particular intends to be aggressive about oversight. And with that I yield back.

Mr. WATT. I appreciate the gentleman's comments and—but I do want to assure him that the Financial Services Committee has had the SEC and a number of these agencies in front of that Committee on a regular basis, so it is not that oversight is not being done. It is being done. And our role, I think, is more on the enforcement side to emphasize not—well, you know, we have got a clear role here, and we just need to not stumble over each over, I guess, is the——

Mr. DELAHUNT. Never enough oversight.

Mr. WATT. Never enough oversight.

Yield back.

Mr. CANNON. I thank the gentleman. Let me also point out that I believe there is never enough oversight, whether it is a Republican administration or a Democrat administration, whether the Republicans control Congress or the Democrats do. That is one of the great, great things about this body. And so to the degree that the Minority has had issues that they want to look at, I hope we have been receptive and are anxious actually to carry out that oversight role. So thank you, Mr. Delahunt, for your kind comments, and Mr. Watt.

Mr. Hillman, if you would like to go ahead, you're recognized for 5 minutes now.

TESTIMONY OF RICHARD J. HILLMAN, DIRECTOR, FINANCIAL MARKETS AND COMMUNITY INVESTMENT, U.S. GOVERNMENT ACCOUNTABILITY OFFICE

Mr. HILLMAN. Thank you, Mr. Chairman. I am pleased to be here today to discuss two recently issued GAO reports that assess SEC's response to trading abuses uncovered in the mutual fund industry. We prepared these reports at the request of Chairman Sensenbrenner and Ranking Member Conyers of the full Committee.

As you know, trading abuses, including fraudulent market timing and late trading violations, were uncovered in many well-known companies in the mutual fund industry and raise significant concerns about the industry's ethical practices. Maintaining public confidence in the mutual fund industry is critical because about 95 million Americans have invested more than 8 trillion in mutual funds, a significant share of the Nation's privately held wealth. Moreover, it is critical that the SEC have the capacity to identify abusive practices and to bring enforcement actions that punish violators and deter those who are contemplating similar abuses.

My written statement today discusses the reasons the SEC did not detect the market timing abuses at an earlier stage, some of the steps that SEC has taken to strengthen its oversight of the mutual fund industry, and enforcement actions taken by SEC and criminal prosecutors in response to these abuses, and SEC's management of procedures related to the making of criminal referrals and ensuring staff independence from the mutual fund industry.

In summary, regarding our first objective, before September 2003, SEC did not examine fund companies for market timing abuses because agency officials, one, viewed other activities as representing much higher risk; two, concluded that companies had financial incentives to control frequent trading because it could lower fund returns; and three, were told by company officials and the companies that they had established controls over frequent trading.

While SEC faced competing examination priorities before September 2003, and had made good-faith efforts to mitigate the known risks associated with legal market timing, lessons can be learned from the Agency not having detected the abuses earlier. First, without paying additional attention to conducting independent assessments of the adequacy of mutual fund company controls, the potential increases that violations may go undetected.

Second, SEC can strengthen its capacity to identify and assess any evidence of potential risk. Information was available to the SEC before these market timing problems were uncovered indicating the possibility of illegal market timing activities. For example, a 2002 study estimated that market timing in certain funds resulted in about 5 billion in annual losses to shareholders and raised the possibility that investment advisors did not always act decisively to control such risks due to potential conflicts of interest.

Third, our review of individual market timing enforcement cases found that compliance staff at mutual fund companies often detected evidence of undisclosed market timing arrangements with favored customers, but lacked sufficient independence within their organizations to correct identified deficiencies. Ensuring the independence of compliance staff is critical, and SEC could potentially benefit from using their work.

Since these abuses were uncovered SEC has acted aggressively to address identified abuses through proposed and final rulemakings, bringing and settling enforcement cases and conducting targeted examinations. In particular, SEC has take a variety of steps to strengthen its mutual fund oversight program and the operations of fund companies, but it is too soon to assess the effectiveness of several key initiatives. For example, SEC has instructed its staff to make additional assessments of company controls and established a new office to improve its capacity to anticipate, identify and manage emerging risks and market trends in the securities industry. SEC also adopted a rule that requires mutual fund companies to appoint independent compliance officers who are to prepare annual reports on their companies' policies and violations; however, SEC has not yet developed a plan to receive and review these annual reports on an ongoing basis and thereby enhance its capacity to detect potential violations.

SEC has agreed with recommendations in our report to strengthen its oversight, including assessing how best to use such compliance reports. At the time of our review, SEC had brought 14 enforcement actions against mutual fund companies and 10 enforcement actions against other firms for mutual fund trading abuses. The penalties obtained in settlements with mutual fund companies are amongst the Agency's highest, ranging from 2 million to 140 million and averaging 56 million. In contrast, penalties obtained in settlements for securities laws violations prior to 2003 were typically under 20 million.

In reviewing a sample of investment advisor cases, we found the SEC followed a consistent process for determining penalties, and that it coordinated penalties and other sanctions with interested parties. However, we found certain weaknesses in SEC's management procedure for making referrals to criminal law enforcement and ensuring staff independence. In particular, SEC does not require staff to document whether a criminal referral was made or why. Without such documentation, SEC cannot readily determine whether staff make appropriate referrals. Further, SEC does not require departing staff to report where they plan to work, information gathered by other financial regulators to assess staff compliance with Federal laws regarding employment with regulated entities. In the absence of such information, SEC's capacity to ensure compliance with these conflict-of-interest laws is more limited.

SEC agreed with our report recommendations to document criminal referrals and employees' postemployment plans.

Mr. Chairman, this completes my prepared statement. I would be happy to respond at the appropriate time to any questions that might arise.

Mr. CANNON. Thank you, Mr. Hillman.

[The prepared statement of Mr. Hillman follows:]

PREPARED STATEMENT OF RICHARD J. HILLMAN

United States Government Accountability Office

GAO

Testimony

Before the Subcommittee on Commercial and Administrative Law, Committee on the Judiciary, House of Representatives

For Release on Delivery
Expected at 4:00 p.m. EDT
Tuesday, June 7, 2005

SEC MUTUAL FUND OVERSIGHT

Positive Actions Are Being Taken, but Regulatory Challenges Remain

Statement of Richard J. Hillman, Director
Financial Markets and Community Investment

GAO

Accountability * Integrity * Reliability

GAO-05-692T

GAO
Accountability · Integrity · Reliability

Highlights

Highlights of GAO-05-692T, a testimony to the Subcommittee on Commercial and Administrative Law, Committee on the Judiciary, House of Representatives

June 7, 2005

SEC MUTUAL FUND OVERSIGHT

Positive Actions Are Being Taken, but Regulatory Challenges Remain

Why GAO Did This Study

Trading abuses—including market timing and late trading violations—uncovered among some of the most well-known companies in the mutual fund industry permitted favored customers to profit at the expense of long-term shareholders. Questions have also been raised as to why the New York State Office of the Attorney General identified the trading abuses in September 2003 before the industry's primary regulator: the Securities and Exchange Commission (SEC). Based on two recently issued GAO reports, this testimony discusses (1) the reasons SEC did not detect the abusive practices at an earlier stage and lessons learned from the agency not doing so, (2) steps the agency has taken to strengthen its mutual fund oversight program, and (3) enforcement actions taken by SEC and criminal prosecutors in response to these abuses and SEC management procedures for making criminal referrals and ensuring staff independence.

What GAO Recommends

Among other steps, the GAO reports recommend that SEC develop a plan to review annual compliance reports on an ongoing basis and document criminal referrals and the post-employment plans of departing staff. SEC generally agreed to implement the reports' recommendations.

www.gao.gov/cgi-bin/getrpt?GAO-05-692T.

To view the full product, including the scope and methodology, click on the link above. For more information, contact Richard J. Hillman at (202) 512-8678 or hillmanr@gao.gov.

What GAO Found

Prior to September 2003, SEC did not examine mutual fund companies for trading abuses such as market timing violations because agency staff viewed other activities as representing higher risks and believed that companies had financial incentives to establish effective controls. While SEC has competing examination priorities, it can draw lessons from not detecting the trading abuses earlier. First, by conducting independent assessments of controls in areas such as market timing (through interviews, reviews of exception reports, reviews of independent audit reports, or transaction testing as necessary), SEC could reduce the risk that violations may go undetected. Second, SEC could further develop its capacity to identify and evaluate evidence of potential risk (for example, academic studies completed between 2000 and 2002 identified certain market timing concerns as a persistent risk to mutual fund customers). Third, ensuring the independence of company compliance staff is critical and SEC staff could better assess company risks and controls through routine interactions with such staff.

SEC has taken several steps to strengthen its mutual fund oversight program and the operations of mutual fund companies, but it is too soon to assess the effectiveness of several key initiatives. For example, SEC has instructed its staff to make additional assessments of company controls and established a new office to identify and assess potential risks. SEC also adopted a rule that requires mutual fund companies to appoint independent compliance officers who are to prepare annual reports on their companies' policies and violations. However, SEC has not developed a plan to receive and review these annual reports on an ongoing basis and thereby enhance its capacity to detect potential violations.

Since September 2003, SEC has brought 14 enforcement actions against mutual fund companies and 10 enforcement actions against other firms for mutual fund trading abuses. Penalties obtained in settlements with mutual fund companies are among the agency's highest—ranging from $2 million to $140 million and averaging $56 million. In contrast, penalties obtained in settlements for securities law violations prior to 2003 were typically under $20 million. In reviewing a sample of investment adviser cases, GAO found that SEC followed a consistent process for determining penalties and that it coordinated penalties and other sanctions with interested states. However, GAO found certain weaknesses in SEC's management procedures for making referrals to criminal law enforcement and ensuring staff independence. In particular, SEC does not require staff to document whether a criminal referral was made or why. Without such documentation, SEC cannot readily determine whether staff make appropriate referrals. Further, SEC does not require departing staff to report where they plan to work, information gathered by other financial regulators to assess staff compliance with federal laws regarding employment with regulated entities. In the absence of such information, SEC's capacity to ensure compliance with these conflict-of-interest laws is limited.

Mr. Chairman, Mr. Ranking Member, and Members of the Subcommittee:

I am pleased to be here today to discuss two recently issued GAO reports that assess the Securities and Exchange Commission's (SEC) response to trading abuses uncovered in the mutual fund industry. We prepared these reports at the request of Chairman Sensenbrenner and Ranking Member Conyers of the full committee.[1] As you know, trading abuses—including fraudulent market timing and late trading violations—were uncovered in many well-known companies in the mutual fund industry and raised significant concerns about the industry's ethical practices.[2] Maintaining public confidence in the mutual fund industry is critical because about 95 million Americans have invested more than $8 trillion in mutual funds, a significant share of the nation's privately held wealth. Moreover, it is critical that SEC and NASD have the capacity to identify abusive practices and to bring enforcement actions that punish violators and deter those who are contemplating similar abuses.[3]

Questions have been raised as to why so many mutual fund companies and broker-dealers were able to engage in trading abuses, sometimes for years, without being detected by SEC and NASD. In fact, the trading abuses only came to light after the New York State Office of the Attorney General (NYSOAG) received a tip from a hedge fund insider, conducted an investigation, and, in September 2003, settled an enforcement action against a hedge fund company and a hedge fund official for market timing

[1]GAO, *Mutual Fund Trading Abuses: Lessons Can Be Learned from SEC Not Having Detected Violations at an Earlier Stage*, GAO-05-313 (Washington, D.C.: April 20, 2005) and *Mutual Fund Trading Abuses: SEC Consistently Applied Procedures in Setting Penalties, but Could Strengthen Certain Internal Controls*, GAO-05-385 (Washington, D.C.: May 16, 2005).

[2]For purposes of this testimony, the term "mutual fund companies" generally refers to mutual fund companies and their related investment advisers and service providers, such as transfer agents, unless otherwise specified. Many mutual fund companies have no employees, although they typically have a board of directors, and rely on investment advisers to perform key functions such as providing management and administrative services.

[3]SEC is the primary regulator of the mutual fund industry. NASD has direct oversight responsibility for broker-dealers that may sell and execute other orders for investment products, including mutual funds.

and late trading of several mutual funds.[1] The federal regulators' failure to identify the abuses at an earlier stage has generated concern about the effectiveness of their examination and other oversight procedures.

As we describe in our reports, market timing and late trading violations permitted favored customers to benefit at the expense of long-term mutual fund company shareholders. Market timing typically involves the frequent buying and selling of mutual fund shares by sophisticated investors, such as hedge funds, that seek opportunities to make profits on the differences in prices between overseas markets and U.S. markets. Although market timing is not itself illegal, frequent trading can harm mutual fund shareholders because it increases transaction costs and lowers a fund's returns. However, market timing can constitute illegal conduct if, for example, it takes place as a result of undisclosed agreements between mutual fund investment advisers (companies that provide management and other services to mutual funds) and favored customers who are permitted to trade frequently and in contravention of stated company trading limits. Late trading, a significant but less widespread abuse than market timing violations, occurs when investors place orders to buy or sell mutual fund shares after the mutual fund has calculated price of its shares, usually once daily at the 4 p.m. Eastern Time close of the financial markets. Investors who are permitted to engage in late trading can profit from the knowledge of events in the financial markets that take place after 4 p.m., an opportunity that other fund shareholders do not have.

My testimony today focuses largely on the market timing area, because such abuses were more widespread than late trading violations, and on SEC, which is the mutual fund industry's frontline regulator. I will discuss late trading issues and NASD oversight activities to a lesser degree. More specifically, my testimony covers (1) the reasons that SEC did not detect the market timing abuses at an earlier stage and lessons learned from the agency not doing so, (2) the steps SEC has taken to strengthen its oversight of the mutual fund industry and strengthen industry business

[1]The term "hedge fund" generally refers to an entity that holds a pool of securities and perhaps other assets that is not required to register its securities offerings under the Securities Act and which is excluded from the definition of investment company under the Investment Company Act of 1940. Hedge funds are also characterized by their fee structure, which compensates the adviser based upon a percentage of the hedge fund's capital gains and capital appreciation. Pursuant to a new rule recently adopted by SEC, advisers of certain hedge funds are required to register with SEC under the Investment Advisers Act of 1940. See Registration Under the Advisers Act of Certain Hedge Fund Advisers, 69 Fed. Reg. 72054 (2004) (to be codified in various sections of 17 C.F.R. Parts 275 and 279).

practices, and (3) enforcement actions taken by SEC and criminal prosecutors in response to these abuses and SEC management procedures related to the making of criminal referrals and ensuring staff independence from the mutual fund industry.

In summary:

Before September 2003, SEC did not examine fund companies for market timing abuses because agency officials (1) viewed other activities as representing higher risks, (2) concluded that companies had financial incentives to control frequent trading because it could lower fund returns, and (3) were told by company officials that the companies had established controls over frequent trading. While SEC faced competing examination priorities before September 2003 and had made good faith efforts to mitigate the known risks associated with legal market timing, lessons can be learned from the agency not having detected the abuses earlier. First, without independent assessments of controls over areas such as market timing during examinations (through interviews, reviews of exception reports, reviews of independent audit reports, or transaction testing as necessary), the risk increases that violations may go undetected. Second, SEC can strengthen its capacity to identify and assess any evidence of potential risks. For example, a 2002 study estimated that market timing in certain funds resulted in about $5 billion in annual losses to shareholders, and raised the possibility that investment advisers did not always act decisively to control such risks due to potential conflicts of interest.[1] Third, we found that compliance staff at mutual fund companies often detected evidence of undisclosed market timing arrangements with favored customers but lacked sufficient independence within their organizations to correct identified deficiencies. Ensuring the independence of compliance staff is critical, and SEC could potentially benefit from using their work.

SEC has taken several steps to strengthen its oversight of mutual fund companies, but it is too soon to assess the effectiveness of certain initiatives. To improve its examination program, SEC staff recently instructed agency staff to conduct more independent assessments of the fund companies' internal controls. To improve its risk assessment capabilities, SEC also has created and is currently staffing a new office to help the agency better anticipate, identify, and manage emerging risks and

[1]Eric Zitzewitz, "Who Cares About Shareholders? Arbitrage-Proofing Mutual Funds," Stanford Graduate School of Business Research Paper No. 1749 (October 2002).

market trends. To better ensure the independence of company compliance staff, SEC recently adopted a rule that requires compliance officers to report directly to the funds' boards of directors. While this rule has the potential to improve fund company operations and is intended to increase the independence of compliance officers, certain compliance officers may still face organizational conflicts of interest. For example, under the rule compliance officers may not work directly for mutual fund companies, but rather, may be employed by investment advisers—who manage the funds—whose interests may not necessarily be fully aligned with mutual fund customers. In addition, although the rule also requires compliance officers to prepare annual reports on their companies' compliance with laws and regulations, SEC has not developed a plan to routinely receive and review the reports. Without such a plan, SEC cannot be assured that it is in the best position to detect abusive industry practices and emerging trends. SEC has agreed to implement recommendations from our April 2005 report to help ensure the effectiveness of compliance officers and to determine how to best utilize the annual compliance reports, or the material findings cited in those reports.

The penalties SEC obtained in the market timing and late trading cases are among the largest in the agency's history and are generally consistent with penalties obtained in cases involving similarly egregious corporate misconduct. As of February 28, 2005, SEC had brought 14 enforcement actions against investment advisers and 10 enforcement actions against other firms for market timing and late trading abuses. It has also brought enforcement actions against several high ranking company officials. Penalties that SEC obtained in settling the 14 enforcement actions with investment advisers range from $2 million to $140 million, with an average penalty of about $56 million. In contrast, penalties obtained in settlements for securities law violations before 2003 were typically under $20 million. In reviewing a sample of cases involving investment advisers, we found that SEC followed a consistent process for determining penalties and that it coordinated penalties and other sanctions with interested states. However, we found certain weaknesses in SEC's overall procedures for referring securities cases to other agencies for potential criminal violations and ensuring that departing employees compiled with conflict-of-interest laws and regulations. SEC has agreed to implement recommendations from our May 2005 report to strengthen these processes.

To address our reporting objectives, we conducted in-depth reviews of 11 SEC enforcement actions against mutual fund companies for market timing and other abusive practices. We reviewed examination reports for these companies as well as related enforcement action documents. We interviewed representatives from SEC, NASD, mutual fund companies, broker-dealers, pension plan administrators, and other industry participants about practices and procedures industry participants use to prevent abuses and monitor trading activity. We also interviewed SEC staff in headquarters and various regional and district offices about how its oversight examination and enforcement efforts were conducted and how penalty amounts were determined. We also obtained information from Department of Justice (DOJ) officials and selected state regulators and attorney generals on criminal enforcement actions brought in cases involving market timing and late trading abuses. In addition, we reviewed relevant academic and other studies. We interviewed SEC staff regarding SEC's management procedures for making criminal referrals to DOJ and state criminal authorities and reviewed related SEC rules. We evaluated these rules using Standards for Internal Controls in the Federal Government.[6] We reviewed federal laws and regulations that govern employees' ability to negotiate and take positions with regulated entities, such as mutual fund companies, and reviewed SEC and other financial regulators' policies and procedures for ensuring staff compliance with these laws. We conducted our work on these reports between May 2004 and May 2005 in accordance with generally accepted government auditing standards.

Lessons Learned from SEC Not Detecting Abusive Market Timing Can Be Useful in Preventing Future Abuses

SEC did not examine for market timing abuses or test company controls in that area, largely because the agency had competing examination priorities and believed that companies had financial incentives to control frequent trading. Lessons learned from SEC not having detected these abuses earlier can be useful to the agency in administering its examination program going forward.

SEC Did Not Examine for Market Timing Abuses

SEC staff have stated that given the number of mutual fund companies, the breadth of their operations, and limited examination resources, SEC's examinations were limited in scope. Examiners focused on discrete areas that staff viewed as representing the highest risks of presenting

[6] GAO, *Standards for Internal Controls in the Federal Government*, GAO/AIMD-00-21.3.1 (Washington, D.C.: 1999).

compliance problems that could impact investors. SEC staff stated that before September 2003, they considered funds' portfolio trading (i.e., purchases and sales of securities on behalf of investors) and other areas as representing higher risks than potential market timing abuses and noted that examinations and enforcement cases in these other areas revealed many deficiencies and violations. SEC staff also said that they did not review market timing controls because they believed that fund companies had financial incentives to control frequent trading because it can lower fund share prices, thereby resulting in a loss of business.[7] An SEC staff member also said that officials from mutual fund companies told agency examiners that they had appointed compliance staff called "market timing police" to enforce compliance with the funds' trading limit policies.

SEC staff said they were surprised in September 2003 when NYSOAG identified the market timing abuses. However, after the abusive practices were identified, SEC moved aggressively to assess the scope and seriousness of the problem. For example, SEC surveyed about 80 large mutual fund companies and determined that nearly 50 percent had some form of undisclosed market timing arrangement with certain customers that appeared to be inconsistent with internal policies, prospectus disclosure, or fiduciary duties. SEC also initiated immediate "cause" examinations and investigations at many of these mutual fund companies to further review potential violations.

I would note that NASD's examinations of broker-dealers also did not discover market timing arrangements involving broker-dealers before September 2003. According to an NASD official, these arrangements went undetected because market timing was not illegal per se and, to the extent that a mutual fund company had stated customer trading limits, broker-dealers may not have perceived themselves as being responsible for enforcing such policies. Regarding late trading, NASD officials said that the organization did not have specific examination guidance to detect the violation before September 2003. NASD officials also said that some broker-dealers created fictitious accounts or otherwise falsified documents, so that detecting late trading violations was difficult.

[7]Since investment adviser fees are often based on the size of assets under management, SEC staff reasoned that companies would establish effective controls to help ensure that assets under management did not decline.

Key Regulatory Lessons Have Emerged from Mutual Fund Trading Abuses

We recognize that SEC faces competing examination priorities and had limited examination resources before September 2003. We also recognize that SEC examiners cannot anticipate every potential fraud, particularly novel frauds such as the undisclosed market timing arrangements between investment advisers and favored customers, such as hedge funds. Further, SEC staff made good faith efforts to control the known risks associated with legal market timing, such as issuing guidance on "fair value" pricing.[8] Nevertheless, three key lessons can be drawn from this experience and used to strengthen SEC's mutual fund oversight program going forward:

- First, performing independent assessments of company controls is essential to confirm views held by regulatory staff regarding risks and the adequacy of controls in place to mitigate those risks. Commonly accepted examination and auditing guidelines call for a degree of professional skepticism in assessing controls (such as mutual fund company market timing controls) and independent verification of their adequacy to mitigate potential risks. Conducting independent testing of controls at a sample of companies, at a minimum, could serve to verify that areas, such as market timing, do in fact represent low risks and that effective controls are in place. A variety of means can be used to independently test controls, including interviewing responsible officials, assessing organizational structure to ensure that compliance staff have adequate independence to carry out their responsibilities, reviewing internal and external audit reports, reviewing exceptions to stated policies, and testing transactions as necessary. If examiners or auditors detect indications of noncompliance with stated policies or requirements, they are expected to expand the scope of their work to determine the extent of identified deficiencies.
- Second, SEC must develop the institutional capacity to identify and evaluate evidence of potential risks and deploy examination staff as necessary to review controls and potentially detect violations in these areas. Our review identified information that was available prior to September 2003 and that was inconsistent with SEC staff's views that market timing was a low-risk area because companies would necessarily act to protect fund returns from the harmful consequences of frequent trading. For example, academic studies indicated that market timing, while legal, remained a persistent risk prior to September 2003 and by one estimate was costing mutual fund shareholders approximately $5 billion

[8] Fair value pricing involves mutual funds using the estimated market value of shares when market quotes are not readily available. Fair value pricing of mutual fund shares can minimize discrepancies between foreign and U.S. markets and thereby minimize market timing opportunities.

annually in certain funds. Further, these studies showed that companies were not acting aggressively to control these risks through fair value pricing, despite SEC's guidance that they do so. The author of a 2002 study raised the possibility that certain investment advisers were not implementing fair value pricing because they were benefiting financially from permitting frequent trading, as turned out to be the case.[9] Moreover, a mutual fund company insider provided information to an SEC district office in early 2003 indicating that a company had poor market timing controls, but the office did not act promptly on this information. If the SEC office had acted on this tip in early 2003, it might have identified potentially illegal market timing activity by company insiders.

- Third, ensuring the independence and effective operation of mutual fund companies' compliance staff is central to preventing violations of the securities laws, regulations, and fund policies. In the majority of the 11 SEC mutual fund company enforcement cases we reviewed, compliance staff lacked such independence. Although the compliance staff—sometimes referred to as "market timing police"—often identified frequent trading that violated company limits, other company officials would routinely overrule the compliance staff's efforts to control such trading. We also found that routine communication with compliance staff could potentially enhance SEC's capacity to detect potential violations at an earlier stage if such staff are forthcoming with relevant information. In cases we reviewed, compliance staff were obviously aware of violations and, in two cases, had documented their findings regarding the harmful consequences of frequent trading in internal company reports. For example, in one case, the sales staff at a mutual fund company overrode the compliance staff's efforts to control hundreds of market timing transactions between 1998 and 2003. In another case, a company's chief compliance officer sent memorandums to the chief executive officer in 2002 and 2003 complaining about the effects of the company's market timing arrangements on long-term shareholders.

[9] Zitzewitz,(2002). Subsequent to September 2003, SEC determined that some favored investors agreed to place assets in mutual funds in exchange for market timing privileges (referred to as "sticky assets"). According to the author, he believed the potential existed that market timers were investing assets in mutual funds, which benefited the related investment advisers because such assets increased their fees.

SEC Has Taken Steps to Strengthen Mutual Fund Oversight, but It Is Too Soon to Assess the Effectiveness of Some Initiatives

SEC has taken several steps over the past two years to strengthen its oversight of the mutual fund industry and improve company practices. These steps include strengthening the agency's mutual fund examination program, establishing an office to better identify emerging risks, hiring additional staff, establishing new tip handling procedures, and enacting a series of rules and rule amendments. Although SEC has taken steps to strengthen its mutual fund company oversight program, it is generally too soon to assess the effectiveness of these initiatives.

To improve its examination program, SEC has instructed examiners to make additional assessments of internal controls at mutual fund companies. For example, SEC staff have identified a range of areas that potentially represent high-risk compliance problems, such as personal trading by company officials, and examiners have initiated independent examinations of these areas. SEC staff also plan to significantly revise the agency's approach to mutual fund company examinations. Rather than evaluating all mutual fund companies on a set cycle as they did between 1998 and 2003, SEC staff plan to begin focusing on the largest and riskiest companies on an ongoing basis. For example, SEC is creating monitoring teams of 2 to 3 individuals who would be responsible for reviewing the largest companies on a more continuous basis, and is placing more emphasis on examinations that target emerging risks. SEC also plans to review some portion of other mutual fund companies on a randomized basis. In a forthcoming report, we assess these and other planned changes to SEC's mutual fund company oversight program. I note that NASD has also recently implemented new examination procedures to better detect market timing and late trading abuses.

SEC also has established the Office of Risk Assessment (ORA) to assist the agency in carrying out its overall oversight responsibilities, including mutual fund oversight. The office's director reports directly to the SEC chairman. According to SEC staff, ORA will enable agency staff to analyze risk across divisional boundaries, focusing on early identification of new or resurgent forms of fraudulent, illegal, or questionable behavior or products. SEC staff said that ORA will seek to ensure that SEC has the information necessary to make better, more informed regulatory decisions. Although ORA may help SEC be more proactive and better identify emerging risks, it is too soon to assess its effectiveness. In this regard, at the close of our review, ORA had established an executive team of 5 individuals but still planned to hire an additional 10 staff to assist in carrying out its responsibilities.

With increased appropriations over recent years, SEC also has hired additional staff to carry out its mutual fund and other oversight programs, potentially enhancing the agency's capacity to test a variety of controls. For example, Office of Compliance Inspections and Examinations staff dedicated to mutual fund company oversight increased by 38 percent between 2002 and 2005 (from 397 to an estimated 547 positions). While the additional staff has the potential to enhance SEC's capacity to oversee key areas within the mutual fund industry, we previously reported that the agency hired the staff without having an updated strategic plan.[10] Without an updated strategic plan in place that identifies the agency's priorities and aligns these priorities with an effective human capital program, it is not clear that SEC's recent hiring decisions will ensure that it has the right amount of resources with the right expertise to do the most effective job possible. In August 2004, SEC revised its strategic plan. We are reviewing SEC's strategic workforce planning as part of a separate engagement.

In addition to hiring staff, SEC has centralized its processes and established new procedures for handling tips and complaints. For example, before the abuses were detected, the agency's Division of Enforcement (Enforcement) had no process under which regional and district office staff would refer complaints and tips to headquarters for review and similarly no process for centralized review of how staff handled complaints and tips. Under the new process, information concerning all enforcement-related tips and complaints, whether received through telephone calls, correspondence, emails, or in-person, is reported to and maintained by a dedicated group within SEC headquarters.

Additionally, SEC has adopted a series of rules and rule amendments designed to strengthen ethical and business practices at mutual fund companies. Among the most significant initiatives, SEC now requires that in order for a mutual fund company to use the agency's exemptive rules, at least 75 percent of its board of directors and the board chair must be independent of the company's investment adviser. [11] SEC believes that increasing boards' independence from investment advisers will help

[10]GAO, *SEC Operations: Oversight of Mutual Fund Industry Presents Management Challenges*, GAO-04-584T (Washington, D.C.: Apr. 20, 2004).

[11]SEC's exemptive rules (i) allow mutual funds to engage in transactions that would otherwise be prohibited under the1940 Act because they present inherent conflicts of interests and (ii) condition the exemptive relief on such transactions being subject to the approval or oversight of independent directors.

prevent the types of trading abuses that we have been discussing today. Further, SEC adopted rules that require mutual fund companies and investment advisers to appoint chief compliance officers (CCO) who are responsible for monitoring compliance with laws and regulations. SEC also requires mutual fund company CCOs to prepare annual reports on company policies and violations.

Although SEC's rulemaking has the potential to strengthen the operations of mutual fund companies and their investment advisers, the incentive structure these rules rely on may not always be sufficient, and further steps may be necessary. More specifically, in our April 2005 report we pointed out that under SEC's rule, fund company CCOs could be investment adviser officials. SEC permitted this arrangement because fund companies often do not have any staff. SEC also believes that it has instituted rules designed to prevent potential conflicts of interest; for example, a mutual fund company's board—including a majority of its independent directors—is solely responsible for removing the CCO. While such steps may mitigate potential conflicts, we recommended that SEC review CCOs' independence as part of the examination process to ensure that those who are advisory firm officials are actually acting independently. SEC agreed with this recommendation. We also pointed out that while SEC examiners planned to review CCO annual reports as part of examinations, the agency has not established a process to receive and review such reports on an ongoing basis. Without such a process, SEC is not in the best position possible to monitor the industry and identify emerging trends. SEC agreed with our recommendation to determine how to best utilize their annual compliance reports, and any material findings cited in those reports.

SEC Consistently Applied Procedures in Setting Mutual Fund Penalties, but Could Strengthen Certain Internal Processes

The penalties that SEC has obtained in enforcement cases related to market timing and late trading violations are among the highest in the agency's history and generally consistent with civil penalties obtained in cases involving similarly egregious corporate misconduct. Additionally, SEC appears to have followed its penalty-setting process consistently in setting penalties in the cases we reviewed. Federal and state prosecutors we contacted said that several factors complicate bringing criminal actions for market timing violations whereas late trading violations are more straightforward to prosecute. We also found certain weaknesses in SEC's overall procedures for referring securities cases to other agencies for potential criminal violations and ensuring that departing SEC employees comply with conflict-of-interest laws and regulations. SEC agreed to implement our recommendations to strengthen these processes.

Penalties in Mutual Fund Trading Abuse Cases Are Among SEC's Highest and Are Consistent with Penalties in Similarly Egregious Cases

Since NYSOAG announced its discovery of the trading abuses in the mutual fund industry in September 2003, SEC has brought 14 enforcement actions against investment advisers primarily for market timing abuses and 10 enforcement actions against broker-dealer, brokerage-advisory, and financial services firms for market timing abuses and late trading. SEC has entered into settlements in all 14 investment adviser cases and obtained penalties ranging from $2 million to $140 million (see fig. 1). These penalties are among the highest SEC has obtained for securities laws violations in its history. Before January 2003, penalties SEC obtained in settlement were generally under $20 million. In contrast, 11 of the 14 penalties obtained in the investment adviser cases are over $20 million, with 8 penalties at $50 million or over. Pursuant to the fair fund provision of the Sarbanes-Oxley Act of 2002 (SOX),[12] SEC plans to use the penalties and disgorgement obtained (disgorgement forces firms to forfeit any ill-gotten gain), a total of about $800 million and $1 billion, respectively, to provide restitution to harmed investors.[13] In addition to settling with investment advisers, as of February 28, 2005, SEC has settled with two broker-dealers, one brokerage-advisory firm, and two insurance companies, with penalties totaling $17.5 million. I note that NASD has taken 12 actions against broker dealers for late trading and market timing abuses with fines and restitutions totaling more than $6 million.

[12]SOX authorizes federal courts and SEC to establish "fair funds" to compensate victims of securities violations. Section 308(a) of SOX provides that if in an administrative or a civil proceeding involving a violation of federal securities laws an order requiring disgorgement is entered, or if a person agrees in settlement to the payment of disgorgement, any penalty assessed against such person may, together with the disgorgement amount, be deposited into a fair fund and disbursed to victims of the violation pursuant to a distribution plan approved by SEC. See Pub. L. No. 107-204, 116 Stat. 745 (2002) (codified in various sections of the United States Code). The "fair fund" provision is codified at 15 U.S.C. § 7246(a).

[13]We are reviewing SEC's implementation of the fair funds provision of SOX as part of a forthcoming report.

Figure 1: SEC Settlements with Investment Advisers for Market Timing Abuses, as of February 28, 2005 (in thousands of dollars)

Investment adviser case[a]	Penalty	Disgorgement	Total
Bank of America Capital Management, LLC[b]	$125,000	$250,000	$375,000
Invesco Funds Group, Inc.	140,000	235,000	375,000
Alliance Capital Management, LP	100,000	150,000	250,000
Massachusetts Financial Services, Co.	50,000	175,000	225,000
Columbia Management Advisors, Inc	70,000	70,000	140,000
Janus Capital Management, LLC	50,000	50,000	100,000
Pilgrim Baxter & Associates, Ltd.	50,000	40,000	90,000
Strong Capital Management, Inc.	40,000	40,000	80,000
Putnam Investment Management, LLC	50,000	5,000	55,000
Banc One Investment Advisors Corporation	40,000	10,000	50,000
PIMCO Advisors Fund Management, LLC	40,000	10,000	50,000
Franklin Advisers, Inc.	20,000	30,000	50,000
RS Investment Management, LP	13,500	11,500	25,000
Fremont Investment Advisors, Inc.[c]	2,000	2,146	4,146
	790,500	1,078,646	1,869,146

Source: SEC.

[a]The entities named in this column are investment advisers associated with these cases. In some cases, SEC simultaneously charged other entities, such as an associated investment adviser, distributor, or broker-dealer for their roles in the market timing abuses. The penalties and disgorgements shown for each case are the totals obtained in settlement from all the entities associated with the case.

[b]Bank of America settled charges involving both abusive market timing and late trading on the part of its investment adviser and broker-dealer subsidiaries, respectively.

[c]Fremont Investment Advisors, Inc. settled charges involving both abusive market timing and late trading.

The penalties SEC obtained in the 14 investment adviser cases are also consistent with penalties obtained in settled enforcement actions in two types of cases that senior Enforcement staff identified as being as egregious as the mutual fund trading abuses—the recent corporate accounting fraud and investment banking conflict-of-interest cases. The recent, large corporate accounting frauds surfaced in late 2000 and concerned publicly traded companies that allegedly used fraudulent accounting techniques to inflate their revenues and drive up stock prices. The investment banking analyst cases involved several investment firms that settled enforcement actions brought by SEC in 2003 for allegedly producing securities research that was biased by investment banking interests. Table 1 compares the range of penalties and average penalties SEC obtained in settled enforcement actions brought against firms for mutual fund trading abuses, corporate accounting fraud, and investment banking conflicts of interest. Although particular penalties reflect the facts and circumstances of each case, table 1 shows that the average penalties among the three types of cases have generally been consistent (when excluding the record $2.25 billion penalty obtained in a corporate accounting fraud case), particularly when compared with the lower penalties obtained in past years. In a public speech, the former Director of Enforcement said that the comparatively large penalties in these cases represented an effort to increase accountability and enhance deterrence in the wake of such extreme misconduct in the securities industry and noted that such penalties create powerful incentives for firms to institute preventative programs and procedures. Others, however, including two members of the Commission, have questioned the appropriateness of these relatively large penalties for public companies, arguing that the cost of penalties are borne by shareholders who are frequently also the victims of the corporate malfeasance.

Table 1: Average Penalties in SEC Settlements with Investment Advisers, Public Companies, and Investment Firms

Case type	Number of settled enforcement actions	Range of penalties	Average penalty
Investment adviser	14	$2—$140 million	$56 million
Public company	11	$3—$250 million, $2.2 billion	$61.5 million[a]
Investment firm	12	$5—$150 million	$43 million

Source: SEC.

[a]The average penalty SEC obtained in settled enforcement actions involving corporate accounting fraud at public companies does not include its record $2.2 billion penalty obtained in its settlement with WorldCom, Inc., in July 2003. A federal district court order stated that the penalty would be satisfied, post bankruptcy, by the company's payment of $500 million in cash and the transfer of common stock in the reorganized company valued at $250 million to a court-appointed distribution agent.

In addition to bringing enforcement actions against firms, SEC has held individuals responsible for their roles in the trading abuses. As of February 28, 2005, SEC had brought enforcement actions against 24 individuals and settled with 18, obtaining penalties and industry bars in all cases (see table 2 for penalties) and disgorgements in some. Almost all of these settled enforcement actions involved high-level executives, including eight chief executive officers (CEO), chairmen, and presidents. The penalties SEC obtained in these settlements ranged from $40,000 to $30 million. The penalties obtained from three individuals are among the four highest in SEC's history—one for $30 million (the highest) and two for $20 million.

SEC also obtained a combined $150 million in disgorgement from these three individuals.[14] In addition, as part of its settlements, SEC permanently barred 5 individuals, including the 3 mentioned above, from association with investment advisers, investment companies, and in some cases other regulated entities, and barred the remaining 13 for various periods from their industries.

[14]SEC obtained an additional $529,000 in disgorgement from five other individuals.

Table 2: Penalties SEC Obtained in Settlement from Individuals Charged in Investment Adviser Cases

Individuals charged, by investment adviser case[a]	Penalty
Strong Capital Management, Inc.	
• Founder and former chairman[b]	$30 million
• Former executive vice-president[b]	$375,000
• Former director of compliance[b]	$50,000
Pilgrim Baxter & Associates, Ltd.	
• Former president	$20 million
• Former chief executive officer (CEO)[b]	$20 million
Invesco Funds Group, Inc.	
• Former CEO	$500,000
• Chief investment officer	$150,000
• National sales manager	$150,000
• Assistant vice president of sales	$40,000
Massachusetts Financial Services, Co.	
• Former president	$250,000
• Former CEO	$250,000
RS Investment Management, LP	
• CEO	$150,000
• Chief financial officer	$150,000
Columbia Management Advisors, Inc.	
• Former portfolio manager	$100,000
• Former chief operating officer	$100,000
• Former national sales manager	$50,000
Banc One Investment Advisors, Corporation	
• Former CEO of related fund	$100,000
Fremont Investment Advisers, Inc.	
• Former CEO	$100,000
Total	**$72,515,000**

Source: SEC

[a]Some individuals charged in the investment adviser cases had more than one title with the investment adviser or with an associated entity, such as the related mutual fund. Unless otherwise indicated, the position indicated refers to the position the individual held with the investment adviser.

[b]SEC permanently barred this individual from association with certain regulated entities, including investment advisers and investment companies.

SEC Consistently Applied Procedures in Setting Penalties

In determining appropriate penalties to recommend to the Commission in the investment adviser cases we reviewed, SEC staff consistently applied criteria that the agency has established. These criteria require SEC to consider such things as the egregiousness of the conduct, the amount of harm caused, and the degree of cooperation and to compare proposed penalties with penalties obtained in similar cases. SEC staff may also consider litigation risks in determining appropriate penalties. For example, if SEC pursues an overly aggressive penalty, a defendant may be less likely to settle, and a judge or other arbitrator may not agree with SEC's analysis and impose a lesser penalty. A range of SEC officials participate in SEC's process for setting appropriate penalties—including the Commissioners—to help ensure that no one individual or small group has disproportionate influence over the final decision. Moreover, SEC has coordinated penalties and disgorgement with state authorities in many of its market timing and late trading cases, although some states obtained additional monetary sanctions.

Several Factors Have Complicated Criminal Prosecution of Market Timing, but State and Federal Authorities Have Brought Criminal Charges in Late Trading Cases

Officials from DOJ, NYSOAG, and the Wisconsin Attorney General's Office told us that they have declined to bring criminal charges for market timing, largely because market timing itself is not illegal. In instituting administrative proceedings in the 14 investment adviser cases discussed above, SEC alleged that the undisclosed market timing constituted securities fraud, conduct expressly prohibited under federal securities laws. According to DOJ officials, although state and federal criminal prosecutors can also seek criminal sanctions for securities fraud, such prosecutions may be more difficult to prove than civil actions. DOJ officials told us that criminal prosecutors must be able to prove beyond a reasonable doubt that the defendant committed fraud, whereas civil authorities generally need only show that a preponderance of the evidence indicated a fraudulent action. According to DOJ and NYSOAG officials, for a variety of reasons their review of cases involving market timing arrangements concluded that they did not warrant criminal fraud prosecutions.[15] For example, in commenting on one case involving an investment adviser's undisclosed market timing arrangement, the Wisconsin Attorney General stated that the risk in trying to convince a jury beyond a reasonable doubt that the particular behavior was criminal

[16]DOJ and NYSOAG officials said that the fact that a criminal case has not been brought against an investment adviser to date for entering into undisclosed market timing arrangements with favored investors does not preclude them from bringing one in the future if they believe the facts and circumstances warrant it.

motivated his office and other state prosecutors to instead pursue a civil enforcement action.

According to a recent law journal article, the ambiguous nature of some funds' prospectus language may have further weakened the ability of federal and state prosecutors to bring criminal charges against investment advisers that allowed favored investors to market time.[16] The article stated that it is often unclear whether and to what extent a fund prohibits market timing. For example, many mutual funds merely "discouraged" market timing to the extent that it caused "harm" to the funds. According to the article, such language is subject to various interpretations as to what constitutes discouraging and what constitutes harm to fund performance. Further, it stated that even prospectus disclosures that allow a specific number of exchanges can be ambiguous because the term "exchange" is subject to various interpretations. Such ambiguities may hamper criminal prosecutors' efforts to prove that the market timing arrangements constituted a willful intent to defraud.[17]

In contrast, NYSOAG and DOJ have brought at least 12 criminal prosecutions against individuals involving late trading violations. In one case, NYSOAG charged a former executive and senior trader of a prominent hedge fund with conducting late trading on behalf of that firm through certain registered broker-dealers in violation of New York's state

[16]Roberto M. Braceras, "Late Trading and Market Timing," *Securities & Commodities Regulation*, vol. 37. no.7 (2004).

[17]On April 16, 2004, SEC adopted amendments to Form N-1A requiring open-ended management investment companies (mutual funds) to disclose in their prospectuses both the risks to shareholders of frequent purchases and redemptions of the mutual fund's shares and the mutual fund's policies and procedures with respect to such frequent purchases and redemptions. If the mutual fund's board has not adopted such policies and procedures, the mutual fund must disclose the specific basis for the board's view that it is appropriate for the mutual fund to not have such policies and procedures. These rules are intended to require mutual funds to describe with specificity the restrictions they place on frequent purchases and redemptions, if any, and the circumstances under which any such restrictions will not apply. See Disclosure Regarding Market Timing and Selective Disclosure of Portfolio Holdings, 69 *Fed. Reg.* 22300 (2004) (amendments to Form N-1A; text of the amendments do not appear in the Code of Federal Regulations). Form N-1A is used by mutual funds to register under the Investment Company Act of 1940 and to file a registration statement under the Securities Act of 1933 to offer their shares to the public.

securities fraud statute.[18] According to DOJ officials, criminal prosecution of late trading is fairly straightforward because the practice is a clear violation of federal securities laws.

Inadequate Documentation Procedures Limit SEC's Capacity to Effectively Manage the Criminal Referral Process

SEC staff said that as state and federal criminal prosecutors were already aware of and generally evaluated the mutual fund trading abuse cases for potential criminal violations on their own initiative, SEC staff did not need to make specific criminal referrals to bring these cases to their attention. However, in the course of our review we found that SEC's capacity to effectively manage its overall criminal referral process may be limited by inadequate recordkeeping. SEC rules provide for both formal and informal processes for making referrals for criminal prosecutions; however, senior Enforcement staff told us that SEC uses only the informal procedures (such as telephone calls to criminal authorities) for making criminal referrals, describing them as less time-consuming and more effective than the more cumbersome formal processes, which involved multiple levels of agency review and approval including review and approval by the Commission. While potentially efficient, SEC's informal procedures do not provide critical management information on the referral process. Specifically, SEC staff do not document referrals or reasons for making them. According to federal internal control standards, policies and procedures, including appropriate documentation, should be designed to help ensure that management's directives are carried out. Without proper documentation, SEC cannot readily determine and verify whether staff make appropriate and prompt referrals. Documentation of referrals might serve as an additional internal indicator of the effectiveness of SEC's referral process and is also important for congressional oversight of law enforcement efforts in the securities industry. In response to a recommendation in our report, SEC agreed to institute procedures requiring the documentation of referrals and the reasons for such referrals.

[18] The defendant pleaded guilty to a violation of New York's Martin Act, General Business Law § 352-c(6). This individual also settled a parallel civil enforcement action instituted by SEC. The SEC settlement order found that this individual willfully aided and abetted and caused violations of SEC Rule 270.22c-1 by engaging in late trading of mutual fund shares on behalf of a hedge fund operator.

SEC Efforts to Encourage Staff Compliance with Federal Conflict-of-Interest Laws On New Employment Do Not Include Tracking Post-SEC Employment Plans

SEC provides training and guidance to its staff on federal laws and regulations regarding employment with regulated entities[19], and also requires former staff to notify it if they plan to make an appearance before the agency.[20] However, SEC does not require departing staff to report where they plan to work as do other financial regulators. According to SEC staff, they have not tracked postemployment information because SEC examiners and other staff are highly aware of employment-related restrictions. SEC staff also said that since agency examiners have traditionally visited mutual fund companies periodically to conduct examinations, they are less likely to face potential conflicts of interest than bank examiners who may be located full-time at large institutions. Nonetheless, as I described earlier, SEC is assigning staff to monitor large mutual fund companies on an ongoing basis. These SEC examination teams would likely have more regular contact with fund management over a potentially longer period of time. In addition, the new SEC rule requiring all mutual fund firms to designate CCOs may increase an existing demand for SEC examiners to fill open positions in the compliance departments at regulated entities. As a result, the potential for employment conflicts of interest might increase. In response to a recommendation in our report, SEC agreed to request that departing employees provide information on where they plan to work and institute procedures (including reviewing examination documentation) if agency staff believe that a departed employee's work products may have been compromised due to interactions with a regulated entity.

[19] Federal laws place restrictions on the postfederal employment of executive branch employees. Specifically, these laws generally prohibit federal executive branch employees from participating personally and substantially in a particular matter that a person or organization with whom the employee is negotiating prospective employment has a financial interest. 18 U.S.C § 208(a). In addition, former senior employees are prohibited for a period of 1 year following federal employment from communicating with or appearing before their former federal employer on behalf of anyone with the intent to influence agency action. 18 U.S.C. § 207(a). This "cooling-off" period is 2 years concerning any matter that was pending under a former employee's official responsibility during the 1 year period prior to termination of federal employment. 18 U.S.C. § 207(b).Violation of either the "seeking employment" or postfederal employment activity restrictions can result in civil and criminal sanctions. 18 U.S.C. § 216.

[20] 17 C.F.R. § 200.735-8(b)(1) requires former SEC staff to file a notice with SEC within 10 days after being employed or retained as the representative of any person outside of the government in any matter in which an appearance before, or communication with, SEC or its employees is contemplated. This rule applies to all former SEC staff for 2 years after leaving the agency.

Observations

The undisclosed market timing arrangements and late trading abuses detected in September 2003 represented one of the most widespread and serious scandals in the history of the mutual fund industry. SEC has determined that undisclosed market timing arrangements, in particular, existed at many large mutual fund companies for as long as 5 years. However, before 2003, SEC did not identify the undisclosed arrangements between investment advisers and favored customers through the agency's oversight process. SEC staff faced competing examination priorities that may have affected its capacity to detect the abusive practices but has taken several recent steps intended to strengthen its mutual fund company oversight program and improve company operations. Several lessons can be drawn from the experience in regard to regulators (1) performing independent assessments of internal controls, (2) having the capacity to identify and evaluate evidence of potential risks, and (3) ensuring the independence of the compliance function at mutual fund companies. Accordingly, our April 2005 report included recommendations to enhance the effectiveness of SEC's mutual fund oversight program and help strengthen fund company operations, which SEC agreed to either implement fully or consider ways to implement them. Although our May 2005 report found that SEC consistently applied its penalty setting procedures in the cases we reviewed, it also identified weaknesses in the agency's procedures relating to the referral of securities cases to other agencies for potential criminal violations and ensuring that departing employees compiled with conflict-of-interest laws and regulations. The report included recommendations to better ensure that these agency responsibilities are being met, which SEC agreed to implement.

Mr. Chairman, this completes my prepared statement. I would be happy to respond to any questions that you may have.

GAO Contacts and Staff Acknowledgements

For further information regarding this testimony, please contact me at (202) 512-8678 or hillmanr@gao.gov, or Wesley M. Phillips, Assistant Director, at (202) 512-5660 or phillipsw@gao.gov. Individuals making contributions to this testimony include Emily Chalmers, Fred Jimenez, Stefanie Jonkman, Marc Molino, David Tarosky, and Anita Zagraniczny.

GAO's Mission

The Government Accountability Office, the audit, evaluation and investigative arm of Congress, exists to support Congress in meeting its constitutional responsibilities and to help improve the performance and accountability of the federal government for the American people. GAO examines the use of public funds; evaluates federal programs and policies; and provides analyses, recommendations, and other assistance to help Congress make informed oversight, policy, and funding decisions. GAO's commitment to good government is reflected in its core values of accountability, integrity, and reliability.

Obtaining Copies of GAO Reports and Testimony

The fastest and easiest way to obtain copies of GAO documents at no cost is through GAO's Web site (www.gao.gov). Each weekday, GAO posts newly released reports, testimony, and correspondence on its Web site. To have GAO e-mail you a list of newly posted products every afternoon, go to www.gao.gov and select "Subscribe to Updates."

Order by Mail or Phone

The first copy of each printed report is free. Additional copies are $2 each. A check or money order should be made out to the Superintendent of Documents. GAO also accepts VISA and Mastercard. Orders for 100 or more copies mailed to a single address are discounted 25 percent. Orders should be sent to:

U.S. Government Accountability Office
441 G Street NW, Room LM
Washington, D.C. 20548

To order by Phone: Voice: (202) 512-6000
TDD: (202) 512-2537
Fax: (202) 512-6061

To Report Fraud, Waste, and Abuse in Federal Programs

Contact:

Web site: www.gao.gov/fraudnet/fraudnet.htm
E-mail: fraudnet@gao.gov
Automated answering system: (800) 424-5454 or (202) 512-7470

Congressional Relations

Gloria Jarmon, Managing Director, JarmonG@gao.gov (202) 512-4400
U.S. Government Accountability Office, 441 G Street NW, Room 7125
Washington, D.C. 20548

Public Affairs

Paul Anderson, Managing Director, AndersonP1@gao.gov (202) 512-4800
U.S. Government Accountability Office, 441 G Street NW, Room 7149
Washington, D.C. 20548

PRINTED ON RECYCLED PAPER

Mr. CANNON. Ms. Richards, you're recognized for 5 minutes.

TESTIMONY OF LORI A. RICHARDS, DIRECTOR, OFFICE OF COMPLIANCE INSPECTIONS AND EXAMINATIONS, U.S. SECURITIES AND EXCHANGE COMMISSION

Ms. RICHARDS. Thank you, Chairman Cannon, Ranking Member Watt, Members of the Committee. I am Lori Richards. I am Director of the SEC's Office of Compliance Inspections and Examinations. Thank you for inviting me to testify here today about the SEC's oversight of the mutual fund industry, the recent mutual fund trading abuses and recent GAO reports.

In the last 21 months, the SEC has moved quickly to implement a series of reforms with respect to mutual funds. We rapidly examined and investigated fund firms and brought numerous enforcement actions. We adopted new rules designed to improve mutual funds governance, ethical standards, compliance and internal controls. We initiated reforms to SEC rules designed specifically to address market timing and late trading. And finally, we improved SEC examiners' ability to detect emerging compliance problems promptly. It is our expectation that, taken together, these reforms will minimize the possibility of these types of abuses from occurring again.

My testimony today focuses primarily on the significant steps that the SEC has taken with respect to its examination oversight of mutual funds. There are now over 8,000 mutual funds managed in over 900 mutual fund complexes, and over 8,000 investment advisors registered with the SEC. The size of the mutual fund industry does not allow the SEC to conduct comprehensive audits of all of their operations. Until recently the SEC had approximately 360 staff people who were dedicated to these examinations. In 2003, however, budget increases allowed us to increase the size of the SEC's examination staff to approximately 500 staff people.

Given the size of the industry, our examinations focus on those areas that, in our view, pose the greatest risk to investors. The challenge for any regulator with limited resources is to identify and to effectively target those areas that pose the greatest risk. SEC examinations are, therefore, focused on the use of a fund investor's assets, their money and their securities, and primarily whether the mutual fund is making investments on behalf of investors that are appropriate, how mutual funds are being marketed and sold to retail investors, and whether funds were trying to inflate the returns of the fund or take on undisclosed risk in order to generate more sales.

It is important for me to note that while market timing was the subject of recent GAO reports, SEC examinations have often detected serious compliance problems in other areas, and those have resulted in serious enforcement actions. For example, the SEC has been on the forefront of discovering and addressing abuses with respect to the widespread failure to deliver mutual fund discounts to investors on their purchases of mutual funds; investment advisors' undisclosed favoritism in the allocation of shares amongst their client accounts; the failure to disclose the use of mutual funds money to pay the cost of selling fund shares; and various types of sales abuses, in particular selling one type of fund to an investor when another type of fund would be better for that particular investor, and various unsuitable sales associated with the sales of variable annuity products.

Since the first instances of market timing and late trading were identified by a tip to the New York Attorney General's Office, the SEC moved very rapidly to investigate this issue in the broader mutual fund industry. As of May 31, 2005, the SEC has brought 29 enforcement actions involving mutual fund complexes and their employees and 12 enforcement actions involving broker-dealers and their employees. The recent GAO report outlined some of these enforcement actions, and recognizes that the penalties obtained in these cases are among the largest ever imposed by the SEC. Prior to 2003, as the GAO report notes, we did not identify the covert secret market timing arrangements between mutual funds and active traders.

It is important to note that there is a difference between market timing that is legal and market timing that is illegal. Illegal market timing involved secret arrangements between fund executives and select market timers. By their nature these were secret, undisclosed arrangements, some of which we now know involved nominee accounts and false trading records. The SEC did not have prior notice of these secret arrangements that some mutual fund executives had with favored traders.

GAO has stated that we can learn lessons from our experience with market timing. I suppose I would recast that statement slightly to say that we have learned lessons from our experience with market timing. We have implemented changes to our examination protocols that will allow examiners not only to detect abusive market timing and late trading, but, perhaps more importantly, to be more nimble, to be more aggressive, to be more proactive in identifying other types of misconduct associated with mutual funds.

The new methodology is described in some detail in my written testimony, but key enhancements include conducting focused routine examinations on the highest-risk firms; increasing the use of data and technology in examinations, including by randomly reviewing mutual fund employees' e-mails. One of the lessons we learned is that the secret market timing arrangements were often negotiated between mutual fund executives and market timers via e-mail communications. So those are now critical aspects of our routine examinations.

We are studying the development of an off-site surveillance program for mutual funds and investment advisors. We implemented a new risk mapping program to better identify areas of emerging risk. We have implemented a new program to rapidly investigate emerging compliance problems by use of sweep examinations. We are implementing dedicated monitoring teams for the largest fund organizations, and, very importantly, to help reduce violations or help eliminate the possibility that violations could occur in the first place. We are reaching out to the new chief compliance officers at mutual fund firms and investment advisors in a new chief compliance officers outreach program to help them better eliminate compliance problems in the first place.

In sum, the SEC has taken aggressive steps to address abusive market timing and late trading in mutual fund shares, but more broadly, the SEC has taken steps to protect investors from the next instance of fraud and abuse by improving our ability to spot emerging problems more quickly.

Thank you, and I am happy to answer any questions you may have.

Mr. CANNON. Thank you.

[The prepared statement of Ms. Richards follows:]

PREPARED STATEMENT OF LORI A. RICHARDS

Testimony Concerning SEC's Mutual Fund Oversight

by Lori A. Richards
Director, Office of Compliance Inspections and Examinations
U.S. Securities & Exchange Commission

Before the U.S. House Subcommittee on Commercial and Administrative Law

June 7, 2005

Chairman Cannon, Ranking Member Watt, and Members of the Subcommittee:

I am Lori Richards, Director of the Securities and Exchange Commission's Office of Compliance Inspections and Examinations ("OCIE"). Thank you for inviting me to testify today on behalf of the SEC about the SEC's oversight of the mutual fund industry, the recent mutual fund trading abuses and recent GAO reports concerning the SEC's examination and enforcement actions with respect to these abuses (GAO-05-313 and GAO-05-385). In the wake of the abuses, the SEC moved quickly to implement a series of mutual fund reforms. The SEC: (1) rapidly examined and investigated fund firms, and brought numerous enforcement actions involving abusive market timing and late trading; (2) adopted new rules designed to improve mutual funds' governance, ethical standards, compliance and internal controls, and disclosures to investors; (3) initiated reforms to SEC rules designed to address market timing and late trading; and (4) improved the ability of the SEC's examination program to detect emerging compliance problems promptly. It is the SEC's expectation that, taken together, these reforms will minimize the possibility of the types of abuses we have witnessed in the past 21 months from occurring again.

I have attached as an appendix a summary of the recent new and proposed new rules with respect to mutual funds, as well as a list of the SEC enforcement actions involving abusive market timing and late trading. My testimony today will focus primarily on the significant steps the SEC has taken with respect to its examination oversight of mutual funds.

I. SEC's Examinations of Mutual Funds

With more than 92 million Americans invested in mutual funds, representing tens of millions of households, and approximately $8 trillion in assets, mutual funds are a vital part of this nation's economy. Millions of investors depend on mutual funds for their financial security.

The SEC staff conducts compliance examinations of mutual funds and investment advisers. There are now some 8,000 funds, managed in over 900 fund complexes, and over 8,000 investment advisers. Until recent years, the SEC had approximately 360 staff persons for these examinations. In 2003, budget increases allowed the SEC to increase its staff for fund examinations by a third, to approximately 500 staff. The size of the mutual fund industry precludes a comprehensive audit of each registrant's operations by examination staff. Staff examinations, therefore, focus on those areas that, in the staff's view, pose the greatest risk to investors.

Examinations identify compliance problems at individual firms, and also help to identify areas of emerging compliance risk in the fund industry generally. Prior to 2003, the focus of SEC examinations was on conflicts of interest in the management of mutual funds, and in particular, whether funds were trying to inflate the returns of the fund, or take on undisclosed risk. The concern was that, in attempting to produce strong investment returns to attract and maintain shareholders, fund portfolio managers and other employees had an incentive to engage in misconduct in the management of the fund. The staff focused on these areas not only because of the risks posed, but also because past examinations had identified problems in these areas, and there was concern that the problems could be more widespread. As a result, examination protocols required that significant attention be focused on portfolio management, order execution, allocation of investment opportunities, pricing and calculation of net asset value, marketing of returns, and safeguarding fund assets from theft. SEC examiners identified a number of practices that can harm investors, including, for example, abusive soft dollar arrangements, favoritism in the allocation of investments, misrepresentations and omissions in the sales of fund shares, inaccurate pricing of fund shares, the failure to obtain best execution in portfolio transactions, sales practice abuses in the distribution of different classes of mutual fund shares, and the failure to give customers the discounts (called "breakpoints") generally available on large purchases of fund shares.

Since the first instances of market timing and late trading at several fund firms were identified by a tip and a subsequent investigation by the New York Attorney General's Office in September 2003, the SEC moved rapidly to investigate this issue in the broader mutual fund industry. The Commission initiated immediate examinations and investigations of a large number of market participants to determine whether they engaged in undisclosed abusive market timing and late trading in fund shares. As of May 31, 2005, the Commission has brought 29 enforcement actions involving mutual fund complexes and their employees, and 12 enforcement actions involving broker-dealers and their employees. The recent GAO report outlines some of these enforcement actions, and recognizes that the penalties obtained in these cases are among the highest imposed by the SEC. The GAO found that the SEC followed a consistent process for determining penalties and that the SEC coordinated penalties and other sanctions with interested state regulators.

Also as part of this study, GAO examined the SEC's criminal referral process. While the SEC does not itself have authority to make criminal prosecutions, working with the criminal authorities is a critical component to effective enforcement of the securities laws. Senior enforcement officials consistently review matters under their responsibility for referrals to criminal authorities. The SEC has delegated to the staff at a senior level, the authority to discuss any matter with the criminal authorities to determine their interest. The staff has also been delegated authority to provide access to any documents to these authorities. The staff works with the criminal authorities on a regular basis, such as on the Corporate Fraud Task Force, and holds regular meetings with U.S. Attorneys Offices and state prosecutors, so that there is an open line of communication and effective relationships have developed. This process, while informal, has proven to be highly effective. In fiscal year 2004, the SEC coordinated with 41 U.S. Attorney's Offices and 8 state prosecutors on 159 indictments or informations for 302 individuals. In the mutual fund trading abuse area the SEC coordinated extensively with the criminal authorities. Criminal authorities are aware of all SEC investigations relating to mutual fund market timing abuses. The criminal authorities have evaluated each of these matters for their appropriateness for a criminal prosecution. GAO has recommended that the SEC track referrals to the criminal authorities and the staff is in the process of converting its case opening form to a web-based application, which will provide for documentation of referrals to criminal authorities.

The GAO notes that prior to September 2003, SEC examination staff did not detect the abusive and secret market timing arrangements that fund executives had with select traders. It is important to note that the illegal market timing involved secret arrangements between fund executives and select market timers allowing the timers to engage in more frequent trading than the fund's prospectus or other internal policies allowed. Some of the arrangements involved nominee accounts and false trading records. These were covert, non-disclosed arrangements. In fact, many fund firms stated at the time that they deterred market timers, and had even hired "market timing police" to prevent this type of trading. The SEC did not have prior notice of these secret arrangements that some mutual fund executives had with favored traders.

It is important to distinguish between the market timing that was illegal (involving covert agreements described above) and the market timing that was not illegal. As the GAO notes, market timing itself is not illegal – traders attempt to "arbitrage" securities held in mutual funds because of the way mutual fund securities are priced each day. Most mutual funds price their shares at 4pm ET, by using the closing market price of the securities in the fund. For securities traded on a foreign exchange, the foreign market may have closed many hours earlier. If an event affecting the value of the portfolio securities occurs after the foreign market closes but before the fund prices its shares, the foreign market closing price for the portfolio security will not reflect the current value of those securities. Traders may attempt to purchase fund securities with knowledge that the prices are "stale" and do not reflect these intervening events. While not illegal, this short term trading may disadvantage the fund's long-term investors by imposing trading costs, disrupting the management of the fund's portfolio and extracting value from the fund.

To help combat frequent trading, the SEC recently adopted rules requiring that mutual funds better disclose their policies with respect to market timing, and allowing mutual funds to impose redemption fees to discourage short-term trading. As GAO notes in its report, the ability to arbitrage mutual funds may also be diminished if mutual funds take steps to "fair value" their securities by updating the price of the security with more current information. The SEC has also taken steps to provide mutual funds with improved ability to effectively enforce their market timing restrictions with respect to those shareholders who purchase fund shares through intermediaries (such as broker-dealers and retirement plan administrators).

GAO stated that the SEC can learn lessons from its experience with market timing. In addition to the regulatory and enforcement actions the Commission has taken, OCIE instituted a number of improvements to the examination process. OCIE implemented changes to our examination protocols that will aid examiners in being able to detect these types of abuses in the future, and importantly, to detect additional types of fraudulent conduct. The challenge for any examination oversight program is to determine how best to use limited resources to oversee a large and diverse industry. More specifically, the challenge is to identify the areas of highest risk to investors, and to probe these areas effectively. Beginning in early 2004, OCIE shifted to a risk-based methodology for examining mutual funds and investment advisers. OCIE spots risks earlier, conduct reviews that are highly focused on identified risks, and report the results of those reviews to the Commission. This new methodology allows the staff to move more quickly, to be more nimble, and to be more responsive to the rapidly changing risk environment in the fund community. This new risk-based approach has involved a number of specific program enhancements, summarized below (key enhancements are described in more detail later in the testimony). SEC examination staff have:

- Focused routine examinations on high-risk firms: with the additional resources added to the examination program in 2003, OCIE increased examination frequency of the largest fund firms, and those fund firms posing the greatest compliance risk (from once every five years, to once every two or three years -- prior to 1998, examination cycles had been as infrequent as once every 12-24 years). Other firms are examined "for cause," in sweeps, or randomly;

- Increased the use of technology and data;

- Implemented a new "Risk Mapping" method to identify new or emerging areas of compliance risk, and worked closely with the SEC's new Office of Risk Assessment to help identify and coordinate areas of risk across the agency;

- Implemented a new program to rapidly investigate emerging compliance problems promptly by use of "sweep examinations;"

- Increased the use of interviews during examinations, as part of the assessment of a firm's control or risk environment;

- Worked with an SEC task force to study the possible use of data as part of a surveillance program for funds and advisers;

- Initiated new dedicated "monitoring team" program for certain large advisers; and

- Initiated a new "Chief Compliance Officer Outreach" program to help new mutual fund and investment adviser chief compliance officers identify and resolve compliance problems at their firms.

As GAO notes in its report, prior to the identification of market timing abuses in 2003, in late 2002, SEC examiners adopted an approach for routine examinations designed to evaluate the quality of fund firms' own internal compliance controls, including by testing those controls in key operational areas. To better detect market timing, in 2003, SEC added a review of a fund's daily sales and redemptions data, which can reveal patterns of trading in a fund's shares that may indicate market timing. Additionally, because the covert arrangements that fund executives had with select shareholders were often evidenced only in e-mail communications and not in written agreements, contracts, or other documents, SEC examiners now frequently request e-mail communications during examinations (past routine examinations did not include a random review of employees' e-mail communications, unless there was cause to believe that particular communications were relevant to the examination). Additional new examination steps include a review of personal trading records showing trading in the fund shares by select fund executives. Previously, SEC rules did not require fund executives to report internally their trading in their fund shares. In July 2004, the SEC closed this loophole, and required that fund executives report all of their trades to fund compliance officials for review. This broader reporting requirement, which had already been adopted by a number of fund groups when the Commission adopted it, is designed to give fund managers a better tool to monitor their employees who might be tempted to market time their own funds.

More broadly, to identify emerging areas of compliance risk promptly, the examination program now includes an extensive "Risk Mapping" exercise. All examiners, from the most junior to the most senior, participate in small focus-group-like discussions about the compliance risks they have perceived in the securities industry. Participants identify risks, map them to relevant mitigating and aggravating conditions, and propose possible compliance and regulatory solutions. The risks are then divided into national risks, those requiring an immediate response across the program, and emerging risks, those requiring attention, but not a full-scale immediate response. In addition to reviewing and testing controls in key high-risk areas, GAO recommends that SEC request lists of all compliance-related reports from fund firms during examinations. The SEC is evaluating this recommendation. Finally, to aid in the effort to identify issues posing risk, examination staff conducts a small number of "wall-to-wall" examinations designed to comprehensively probe fund operations to assist in detecting areas of emerging compliance risk that may not be indicated by other means.

The examination program now includes risk-targeted sweeps. In a risk-targeted sweep, staff review a risk or potential violation across a number of different firms. In terms of methodology, this is a "horizontal" review. That is, staff look at the risk area across several firms, as compared to a "vertical" review where it would look at a single firm from top to bottom. Risk targeted sweeps provide several important advantages. As soon as a developing risk is identified, an examination team is deployed to look into it. In many cases OCIE begins with a small sample of firms. If the risk appears serious OCIE may expand the size of the sample, and include more firms. When completed, OCIE has examination results from a defined sample of firms that have been visited in a roughly contemporaneous period of time. This allows OCIE to make sound inferences about the nature and danger of the risk in the industry generally. As an example of this examination technique, the SEC recently released our findings from a risk-targeted examination sweep of investment advisers that provide advice to pension plans, focusing on disclosure and conflicts of interest (available at http://www.sec.gov/news/studies/pensionexamstudy.pdf).

Finally, OCIE continues to develop additional program enhancements. For example, OCIE's examination program will soon include monitoring teams for the largest mutual fund complexes. Teams of examiners will be assigned to each mutual fund group, will get to know the business and operations of the complex, and will visit it regularly.

The SEC is also exploring ways to better spot indications of aberrant conduct outside of the examination process. Chairman Donaldson formed an SEC staff task force to study surveillance of advisers and funds and to explore how the staff can enhance its oversight of the industry. The goal of such a surveillance program would be to identify indications of problems, and then target the particular fund or adviser for follow up inquiry by telephone, letter, or on-site visit. Staff would also be able to examine the relevant data -- industry-wide -- to determine if a systemic problem is emerging. Surveillance systems already protect other significant classes of financial assets and the task force is exploring whether similar surveillance can be deployed to protect those who invest in mutual funds or entrust their money to investment advisers.

More fundamentally, the SEC has recently put new rules into place that are designed to improve compliance by funds and advisers by requiring that they strengthen their own internal compliance programs. The new rules require that advisers and funds implement and maintain written compliance policies and procedures designed to prevent, detect, and correct compliance problems in key areas of their operations. The new rules also require that funds and advisers designate a chief compliance officer to implement those compliance policies and procedures, and, in order to assist the fund board in exercising compliance oversight, that fund's chief compliance officer report on compliance matters to the fund's board of directors. GAO has recommended that SEC examinations seek to assess the "independence and effectiveness" of these new chief compliance officers during examinations. Consistent with this recommendation, OCIE has been assessing their role since the new rule went into effect last October, and is preparing guidance for SEC exam staff. GAO suggested that the SEC develop a plan to receive and review funds' annual compliance reports to their boards of directors on an ongoing basis. The staff is considering this recommendation.

Finally, GAO suggested that the SEC enhance its procedures to avoid ethical conflicts of interest, especially by examiners who leave the SEC to work for a private firm. The SEC has worked to establish and maintain the highest levels of ethics and integrity across the agency. Within the examination program, in 1997 the staff developed a series of ethics guidelines for examiners that exceed the standards of the Office of Government Ethics. These guidelines are intended to assure staff independence in conducting examinations. They include guidance on how to avoid conflicts of interest while examining a registrant, what to do when seeking employment outside the SEC, how to handle personal conflicts, how to address situations where employment or relationships with a spouse or personal friend creates a potential conflict, and numerous other issues. SEC staff also receive training on ethics, including periodic refresher courses specifically for examiners. OCIE recently instituted several enhancements to the ethics program. OCIE now has at least one ethics official in the examination program of each of the SEC's regional and district offices to provide advice and guidance to examination staff on issues they encounter, and special training sessions are planned for these new ethics officials. Finally, as GAO suggested, the SEC is in the process of establishing a process for requesting information from departing staff regarding the individual's new employer.

We also strongly believe in vigorously continuing our outreach program to the industry. It is important that the industry understand the concerns of the Commission and our examination approach. It is also vitally important that we receive input and feedback from the industry about our process.

II. Conclusion

In sum, the SEC has taken aggressive steps to address abusive trading in mutual fund shares, to detect abusive conduct and more broadly, to improve funds' compliance programs to protect investors.

Thank you. I would be pleased to answer any questions you may have.

ATTACHMENT

SEC Mutual Fund Initiatives

For informal, informational purposes only.
Prepared by the SEC's Office of Legislative Affairs
Consists primarily of information found in SEC press releases.
For complete information, please refer to official SEC postings on www.sec.gov

COMMISSION ACTIONS:

Amendments to Rules Governing Pricing of Mutual Fund Shares – Late Trading
On **December 3, 2003**, the Commission proposed a rule requiring that fund orders be received by 4:00 p.m. Specifically, this proposal would require that an order to purchase or redeem mutual fund shares be received by the mutual fund — or its primary transfer agent or a registered securities clearing agency — by the time that the fund establishes for calculating its net asset value in order to receive that day's price (typically 4:00 p.m. for most funds). This rule would effectively eliminate the potential for late trading through intermediaries that sell fund shares. Comment period ended on February 6, 2004.

- *Press Release:* http://www.sec.gov/news/press/2003-168.htm
- *Proposed Rule:* http://www.sec.gov/rules/proposed/ic-26288.htm

Disclosure Regarding Market Timing and Selective Disclosure of Portfolio Holdings
On **December 3, 2003**, the Commission proposed enhanced disclosure requirements for mutual funds. Funds would be required to disclose: (1) market timing policies and procedures, (2) practices regarding "fair valuation" of their portfolio securities and (3) policies and procedures with respect to the disclosure of their portfolio holdings. This type of explicit disclosure will shed light on market timing and selective disclosure of portfolio holdings so that investors can better understand the fund's policies and how funds manage the risks in these areas. Comment period ended on February 6, 2004.
Final Rule adopted by the Commission on April 13, 2004.

- *Press Release:* http://www.sec.gov/news/press/2003-168.htm
- *Proposed Rule:* http://www.sec.gov/rules/proposed/33-8343.htm
- *Final Rule:* http://www.sec.gov/rules/final/33-8408.htm

Compliance Programs of Investment Companies and Investment Advisers
On **December 3, 2003**, the Commission **voted to adopt** rules that will require funds and advisers to: (1) have compliance policies and procedures, (2) annually review them and (3) designate a chief compliance officer who, for funds, must report to the board of directors. Designated compliance officers and written policies and procedures will have several benefits, including having a designated person charged with fund compliance who must answer to, and be accountable to, the fund's board of directors, thereby enhancing compliance oversight by directors, as well as allowing the SEC's examination staff to review the reports made to the board.

- *Press Release:* http://www.sec.gov/news/press/2003-168.htm
- *Final Rule:* http://www.sec.gov/rules/final/ia-2204.htm

Enhanced Disclosure of Breakpoint Discounts by Mutual Funds
On **December 17, 2003**, the Commission proposed amendments that would require a mutual fund to provide enhanced disclosure regarding breakpoint discounts on front-end sales loads. This enhanced disclosure will assist investors in understanding the breakpoint opportunities available to them. Comment period ended on February 13, 2004.
Final Rule adopted by the Commission on May 26, 2004.

- *Press Release:* http://www.sec.gov/news/press/2003-173.htm
- *Proposed Rule:* http://www.sec.gov/rules/proposed/33-8347.htm
- *Final Rule:* http://www.sec.gov/rules/final/33-8427.htm

Concept Release on Mutual Fund Transaction Costs
On **December 17, 2003**, the Commission issued a concept release on mutual fund transaction costs. The release seeks public comment on whether mutual funds should be required to quantify and disclose to investors the amount of transaction costs they incur; include transaction costs in their expense ratios and fee tables; provide other measures or additional disclosure that would indicate the level of a fund's transaction costs; or some combination of the above. Comment period ended on February 23, 2004.

- *Press Release:* http://www.sec.gov/news/press/2003-173.htm
- *Concept Release:* http://www.sec.gov/rules/concept/33-8349.htm

New Investment Company Governance Requirements
On **January 14, 2004**, the Commission voted to propose amendments to its rules to enhance fund boards' independence and effectiveness and to improve their ability to protect the interests of the funds and fund shareholders they serve. The proposed fund governance standards include: (1) Independent Composition of the Board, (2) Independent Chairman of the Board, (3) Annual Self-Assessment of Board, (4) Separate Meetings of Independent Directors, (5) Independent Director Staff and (6) Preservation of Documents regarding Reasonableness of Fees. Comment period ended on March 10, 2004. **Final Rule adopted by the Commission on June 23, 2004.**

- *Press Release*: http://www.sec.gov/news/press/2004-5.htm
- *Proposed Rule*: http://www.sec.gov/rules/proposed/ic-26323.htm
- *Final Rule*: http://www.sec.gov/rules/final/ic-26520.htm

Investment Adviser Codes of Ethics and Insider Reporting of Fund Trades
On **January 14, 2004**, the Commission voted to propose new rules and related rule amendments under the Investment Advisers Act of 1940. The new rule would require registered investment advisers to adopt and enforce codes of ethics applicable to their supervised persons and, for advisers to funds, to require insiders to report their trades in fund shares. Comment period ended on March 15, 2004. **Final Rule adopted by the Commission on May 26, 2004.**

- *Press Release:* http://www.sec.gov/news/press/2004-5.htm
- *Proposed Rule:* http://www.sec.gov/rules/proposed/ia-2209.htm
- *Final Rule:* http://www.sec.gov/rules/final/ia-2256.htm

Confirmation Requirements and Point of Sale Disclosure Requirements for Mutual Fund Transactions
On **January 14, 2004**, the Commission voted to propose new rules that are designed to enhance the information that broker-dealers provide to their customers in connection with transactions in certain types of securities. The two new rules would require broker-dealers to provide their customers with targeted information regarding the costs and conflicts of interest that arise from the distribution of mutual fund shares. The rules would require disclosure at two key times - first at the point of sale, and second at the completion of a transaction in the transaction confirmation. Comment period ended on April 12, 2004. On **March 1, 2005**, the Commission announced that it has reopened the comment period for and requested supplemental comments on the proposed rule. The supplemental release reflects issues raised by commenters to our initial proposal, including investor feedback from in-depth testing of prototype disclosure forms.

- *Press Release*: http://www.sec.gov/news/press/2004-5.htm
- *Proposed Rule*: http://www.sec.gov/rules/proposed/33-8358.htm
- *See also*: Attachments 1-5, Form Examples http://www.sec.gov/rules/proposed/33-8358_attach.pdf
- *Supplemental Release*: http://www.sec.gov/rules/proposed/33-8544.pdf
- *See also*: Supplemental Release Attachment, Form Examples http://www.sec.gov/rules/proposed/33-8544attach.pdf

Enhanced Mutual Fund Expense and Portfolio Disclosure
On **February 11, 2004**, the Commission **adopted** several amendments to its rules and forms that are intended to improve significantly the periodic disclosure that mutual funds and other registered management investment companies provide to their shareholders about their costs, portfolio investments, and performance. The amendments included the following: Enhanced Mutual Fund Expense Disclosure in Shareholder Reports; Quarterly Disclosure of Fund Portfolio Holdings; Use of Summary Portfolio Schedule; Exemption of Money Market Funds from Portfolio Schedule Delivery Requirements; Tabular or Graphic Presentation of Portfolio Holdings in Shareholder Reports; and Management's Discussion of Fund Performance. The new requirements will apply to shareholder reports and quarterly portfolio disclosure for reporting periods ending on or after 120 days following publication in the *Federal Register*.

- *Press Release*: http://www.sec.gov/news/press/2004-16.htm
- *Proposed Rule*: http://www.sec.gov/rules/proposed/ic-25870.htm
- *Final Rule:* http://www.sec.gov/rules/final/33-8393.htm

Improved Disclosure of Board Approval of Investment Advisory Contracts

On **February 11, 2004**, the Commission proposed amendments to its rules and forms that would improve the disclosure that mutual funds and other registered management investment companies provide to their shareholders regarding the reasons for the fund board's approval of an investment advisory contract. The proposals are intended to encourage fund boards to consider investment advisory contracts more carefully and to encourage investors to consider more carefully the costs and value of the services rendered by the fund's investment adviser. The proposals would require fund shareholder reports to discuss, in reasonable detail, the material factors and the conclusions with respect to these factors that formed the basis for the board of directors' approval of any investment advisory contract. Comment period ended on April 26, 2004. **Final Rule adopted by the Commission on June 23, 2004.**

- *Press Release*: http://www.sec.gov/news/press/2004-16.htm
- *Proposed Rule*: http://www.sec.gov/rules/proposed/33-8364.htm
- *Final Rule*: http://www.sec.gov/rules/final/33-8433.htm

Prohibition on the Use of Brokerage Commissions to Finance Distribution

On **February 11, 2004**, the Commission proposed an amendment to rule 12b-1 under the Investment Company Act of 1940 that would prohibit open-end investment companies (mutual funds) from directing commissions from their portfolio brokerage transactions to broker-dealers to compensate them for distributing fund shares. The Commission also is requesting comment on the need for additional changes to rule 12b-1 to address other issues that have arisen under the rule. Comment period ended on May 10, 2004. **Final Rule adopted by the Commission on August 18, 2004.**

- *Press Release*: http://www.sec.gov/news/press/2004-16.htm
- *Proposed Rule*: http://www.sec.gov/rules/proposed/ic-26356.htm
- *Final Rule*: http://www.sec.gov/rules/final/ic-26591.htm

Redemption Fees for Mutual Fund Securities

On **February 25, 2004**, the Commission voted to propose new Rule 22c-2 under the Investment Company Act of 1940. This rule would require all mutual funds to impose a 2 percent fee on the redemption proceeds of shares redeemed within 5 days of their purchase. The rule is designed to require short-term shareholders to reimburse the fund for the direct and indirect costs that the fund pays to redeem these investors' shares. In the past, these costs generally have been borne by the fund and its long-term shareholders. The rule would supplement other measures the Commission has recently taken to address short-term trading, including abusive market timing activity. Comment period ended on May 10, 2004. On **March 3, 2005**, the Commission voted to adopt new Rule 22c-2 under the Investment Company Act of 1940. The rule will require the boards of mutual funds that redeem shares within 7 days to adopt a redemption fee of no more than 2 percent of the amount of the shares redeemed or determine that a redemption fee is not necessary or appropriate for the fund. **Final Rule adopted by the Commission on March 3, 2005.**

- *Press Release*: http://www.sec.gov/news/press/2004-23.htm
- *Proposed Rule*: http://www.sec.gov/rules/proposed/ic-26375a.htm

Disclosure Regarding Portfolio Managers of Registered Management Investment Companies

On **March 11, 2004**, the Commission voted to propose amendments to its forms that are designed to improve the disclosure that mutual funds and other registered management investment companies provide about their portfolio managers. These proposals are intended to provide greater transparency regarding portfolio managers, their incentives in managing a fund, and the potential conflicts of interest that may arise when they also manage other investment vehicles. Comment period ended on May 21, 2004. **Final Rule adopted by the Commission on August 18, 2004.**

- *Press Release*: http://www.sec.gov/news/press/2004-31.htm
- *Proposed Rule*: http://www.sec.gov/rules/proposed/33-8396.htm
- *Final Rule*: http://www.sec.gov/rules/final/33-8458.htm

<u>SEC Civil Actions and Administrative Proceedings Regarding Market Timing and Late Trading in Mutual Funds</u>

Civil Action / Administrative Proceeding	Date Filed	Judgment or Decision	Release No.
In the Matter of Theodore Charles Sihpol III	9/16/2003	Pending	33-8288
In the Matter of Steven B. Markovitz	10/2/2003	10/2/2003	33-8298
In the Matter of James Patrick Connelly Jr.	10/16/2003	10/16/2003	33-8304
SEC v. Justin M. Scott and Omid Kamshad (D. Mass)	10/28/2003	Pending	LR-18428
In the Matter of Putnam Investment Management, LLC	10/28/2003	11/13/2003 4/8/2004	IA-2192, IA-2226
SEC v. Martin J. Druffner, et al. (D. Mass.)	11/4/2003	Pending	LR-18784
SEC v. Invesco Funds Group, Inc. and Raymond R. Cunningham (D. Colo.); <u>settled administratively</u>:	12/2/2003		LR-18482
In the Matter of Invesco Funds Group, Inc., AIM Advisors, Inc., and AIM Distributors, Inc.		10/8/2004	34-50506
In the Matter of Raymond R. Cunningham		10/8/2004	34-50507
SEC v. Mutuals.com, Inc., et al. (N.D. Tex.)	12/4/2003	Pending	LR-18489
In the Matter of Alliance Capital Management, L.P.	12/18/2003	12/18/2003	IA-2205A
SEC v. Daniel Calugar and Security Brokerage, Inc. (D. Nev.)	12/22/2003	Pending	LR-18524
SEC v. Gary L. Pilgrim, Harold J. Baxter, and Pilgrim Baxter & Associates, Ltd. (E.D. Pa.); <u>settled administratively</u>:	11/20/2003		LR-18474
In the Matter of Pilgrim Baxter & Associates, Ltd.		6/21/2004	IA-2251
In the Matter of Gary L. Pilgrim		11/17/2004	33-8505
In the Matter of Harold J. Baxter		11/17/2004	33-8506
SEC v. Security Trust Company, N.A., Grant D. Seeger, William A. Kenyon, and Nicole McCermott (D. Ariz.)	11/25/2003	Pending	LR-18479
(Civil Judgment as to Nicole McDermott)		3/3/2004	LR-18606
(Civil Judgment as to Security Trust Co., N.A.)		3/31/2005	LR-18653
In the Matter of Paul A. Flynn	2/3/2004	Pending	33-8360
In the Matter of Massachusetts Financial Services Co., John W. Ballen, and Kevin R. Parke	2/5/2004	2/5/2004	IA-2213
SEC v. Columbia Management Advisors, Inc. and Columbia Funds Distributor, Inc. (D. Mass.); <u>settled administratively</u>:	2/24/2004		LR-18590
In the Matter of Columbia Management Advisors, Inc. and Columbia Funds Distributor, Inc.		2/9/2005	33-8534

Civil Action / Administrative Proceeding	Date Filed	Judgment or Decision	Release No.
SEC v. PIMCO Advisors Fund Management LLC, et al. (S.D.N.Y.); settled administratively as to the entities, action continues against Stephen J. Treadway and Kenneth W. Corba:	5/6/2004	Pending	LR-18697
In the Matter of PA Fund Management LLC, PEA Capital LLC, and PA Distributors LLC		9/13/2004	34-50354
In the Matter of Strong Capital Management, Inc., et al.	5/20/2004	5/20/2004	34-49741; 34 51694
SEC v. Geek Securities, Inc., Geek Advisors, Inc., Kautilya "Tony" Sharma, and Neal R. Wadhwa (S.D. Fla.)	6/4/2004	Pending	LR-18738
(Civil Judgment as to Neal R. Wadhwa)		10/14/2004	LR-18938
In the Matter of Neal R. Wadhwa		11/5/2004	34-50644
In the Matter of Banc One Investment Advisors Corporation and Mark A. Beeson	6/29/2004	6/29/2004	IA-2254
In the Matter of Franklin Advisers, Inc.	8/2/2004	8/2/2004	IA-2271
In the Matter of CIHC, Inc., Conseco Services, LLC, and Conseco Equity Sales, Inc.	8/9/2004	8/9/2004	33-8455
In the Matter of Inviva, Inc. and Jefferson National Life Insurance Co.	8/9/2004	8/9/2004	33-8456
In the Matter of Janus Capital Management, LLC	8/18/2004	8/18/2004	IA-2277
SEC v. JB Oxford Holdings, Inc. et al. (C.D. Cal.)	8/25/2004	Pending	LR-18850
In the Matter of Michael D. Legoski	8/30/2004	8/30/2004	34-50289
In the Matter of Thomas A. Kolbe	8/30/2004	8/30/2004	IA-2288
In the Matter of Timothy J. Miller	8/30/2004	8/30/2004	IA-2289
In the Matter of Charles Schwab & Co., Inc.	9/14/2004	9/14/2004	34-50360
In the Matter of RS Investment Management Inc, RS Investment Management, L.P., Randall Hecht, and Steven M. Cohen	10/6/2004	10/6/2004	IA-2310
In the Matter of Fremont Advisors, Inc.	11/4/2004	11/4/2004	IA-2317
In the Matter of Nancy C. Tengler	11/4/2004	11/4/2004	IA-2318
In the Matter of Larry Adams	11/4/2004	5/19/2005	IA-2388
In the Matter of Southwest Securities, Inc., Daniel R. Leland, Kerry M. Rigdon, and Kevin J. Marsh	1/10/2005	1/10/2005	34-51002
SEC v. Scott B. Gann and George B. Fasciano (N.D. Tex.)	1/10/2005	Pending	LR-19027
In the Matter of Lawrence S. Powell and Delano N. Sta.Ana	1/11/2005	1/11/2005	34-51017
In the Matter of Banc of America Capital Management, LLC, et al.	2/9/2005	2/9/2005	33-8538
In the Matter of Erik Gustafson	2/9/2005	2/9/2005	IA-2354
In the Matter of Joseph Palombo	2/9/2005	2/9/2005	IA-2352
In the Matter of Peter Martin	2/9/2005	2/9/2005	33-8537
In the Matter of Breen Murray & Co.	2/17/2005	2/17/2005	34-51219
In the Matter of John D. Carifa	4/28/2005	4/28/2005	IA-2379
In the Matter of Gerald T. Malone	4/28/2005	4/28/2005	IA-2378
In the Matter of Michael J. Laughlin	4/28/2005	4/28/2005	34-51624

Mr. CANNON. Secretary Galvin.

TESTIMONY OF WILLIAM FRANCIS GALVIN, SECRETARY OF THE COMMONWEALTH OF MASSACHUSETTS

Mr. GALVIN. Thank you, Mr. Chairman.

Chairman Cannon, Ranking Member Watt, distinguished Members of the Committee, thank you very much for having me here this afternoon. I am Bill Galvin. I'm the Secretary of the Commonwealth of Massachusetts and its chief securities regulator. Among the duties of my office are protecting investors in the Commonwealth of Massachusetts through our securities division.

I am here today to offer my perspective on mutual fund trading abuses, and more specifically this recent April 2005 GAO report. The subtitle of this report is, quote, Lessons Can Be Learned from the SEC Not Having Detected Violations at an Earlier Stage, close quote. From my perspective, the lessons are pretty simple. In the past the SEC simply didn't do it's job. It dropped the ball. It ignored warning signs and inexplicably didn't follow up on tips. In short, it failed to protect mutual fund investors.

Let me be blunt. Had the SEC done what it was supposed to do, we probably wouldn't be here today. Unfortunately, it's not the first time the SEC has let investors down. Consider the history from just the past 10 years. Almost every major enforcement action or investor protection issue was first brought or raised not by the SEC or the NASD, but by State securities regulators. These include penny stock and microstock fraud, day trading abuses, misleading Internet brokerage advertising, analyst conflict of interest matters, and lastly mutual fund trading abuses. In virtually every case the States took the lead.

The revelations of recent years about the securities industry teach an even more compelling lesson, and that is the critical importance of what goes on in what I will call the risk marketplace for average Americans. Their savings, their pensions, their children's education funds, in short their financial futures are now as never before in play in this marketplace.

The GAO report is fine as far as it goes, but it leaves out the most important lesson, in my view, and that is the vital role played by State securities regulators. We need more cops on the securities beat and more constructive competition among them to protect the investing public. Our regulatory monopoly is as bad as any other kind of monopoly. Customers and investors are ill served by monopolies. Monopoly regulators, like monopoly companies, get complacent. They miss things. They can get too cozy with the folks they're supposed to regulate.

I have seen how it works in the securities industry. The regulators and the regulated go to each others' conferences, usually in nice places like Palm Beach and Palm Desert. The revolving door through which Federal regulators go to find lucrative jobs on Wall Street should be the subject of another hearing perhaps on another day.

As I said, we probably wouldn't be here today if the SEC had done its job. Unfortunately it did not. From my perspective as a State securities regulator, I think the SEC has to be aggressive across the board.

Chairman William Donaldson has made some important progress during his time at the Commission. The pending nomination of Mr. Cox and other anticipated vacancies at the SEC raises a most serious question. Is the era of reform and vigorous enforcement over? There is no doubt we are at a crossroads. Just 2 years ago this House of Representatives voted by a margin of 418 to 2 to reform the mutual fund industry. The bill died in the Senate. Was that just for show, or are we serious about giving average Americans real protection?

Over the years the SEC has been criticized for not being proactive and tough enough. I think it is a fair criticism. Traditionally one of the weakest and most toothless divisions of the SEC was in investment management. It has not been known for aggressive examinations, and certainly not for enforcement actions. I'd even call it a regulatory backwater. This is strange and unacceptable, given that nearly 100 million Americans entrust their money to the mutual fund industry. Yet here we have a regulator that ignored reports from academics and even anonymous tipsters from within the industry that market timing was costing investors billions of dollars.

This chicanery and fraud would likely still be going on if it were not for a couple of State securities divisions that acted when the SEC and the NASD did not, despite having a tiny fraction of the resources these two organizations have. In Massachusetts, for example, we brought many—several market timing and late trading enforcement actions based on the tips we received and the exams we conducted. These involved Putnam Mutual Funds, Prudential Securities, Franklin-Templeton and A.G. Edwards. Like State securities regulators across the country who follow up on tips, we answer the phone, we listen to investors, and we're easy to reach.

There are those who would like to see the State securities regulators just go away. They argue our complementary system of State and industry self-regulation is burdensome and duplicative. It is neither. Quite the contrary, it serves to protect investors. The mutual fund trading abuse described in the GAO report are proof of that.

Our system works. That's the lesson of all this. So next time some free market think tank underwritten by Wall Street money says we don't need State securities regulators, that the industry can regulate itself just fine out of enlightened self-interest, you have a simple four-word answer, which also happens to be the title of this report: Mutual Fund Trading Abuses.

The fact is we need more, not fewer, cops on the securities beat. That is the lesson of this scandal. And we need cooperation among regulators, not corruption. We need to check each other's work. Sometimes we need to backstop each other.

A few years ago in 1996, in the name of so-called regulatory reform and efficiency, the States were essentially preempted from the regulation of mutual funds. The scandal we are here today to discuss is a legacy of that misguided policy. Investor protection, including aggressive enforcement of State and Federal securities laws, isn't a partisan issue. Democrats, Republicans, Libertarians, Greens and Independents, we all rely on our Nation's securities markets for financial security. Investors vote, and they are a very large constituency. They need to be protected, and they're relying on us. We must make sure that they are protected.

To sum up, the lessons of this chapter on Wall Street history are simple. While SEC and the NASD dropped the ball, the States picked it up. Our system worked. Now we are about to write the next chapter. Will it be back to business as usual, or will it be real protections for the hard-earned money that our citizens have invested? The answer is up to us.

Thank you very much, Mr. Chairman. I will be happy to answer any question at the appropriate time.

Mr. CANNON. Thank you, Mr. Secretary.

[The prepared statement of Mr. Galvin follows:]

PREPARED STATEMENT OF WILLIAM FRANCIS GALVIN

Chairman Cannon, Ranking Member Watt, and distinguished members of the committee.

My name is William Galvin. I am Secretary of the Commonwealth of Massachusetts and the Chief Securities Regulator.

Among the duties of my office are protecting investors in the Commonwealth through the Securities Division.

I'm here today to offer my perspective on mutual fund trading abuses and, more specifically, this April 2005 GAO report.

The subtitle of this report is "Lessons Can Be Learned from SEC Not Having Detected Violations at an Earlier Stage."

From my perspective, the lessons are pretty simple.

In the past, the SEC simply didn't do its job. It dropped the ball. It ignored warning signs and, inexplicably, didn't follow up on tips. In short, it failed to protect mutual fund investors.

Let me be blunt: Had the SEC done what it was supposed to do, we probably would not be here today.

Unfortunately, it's not the first time the SEC has let investors down. Consider the history from just the past 10 years.

Almost every major enforcement action or investor protection issue was first brought or raised not by the SEC or NASD but by state securities regulators.

- Penny stock and microcap stock fraud
- Day trading abuses
- Misleading Internet brokerage advertising
- Analyst conflicts of interest
- Mutual fund trading abuses

In virtually every case, the states took the lead.

The revelations of recent years about the securities industry—teach an even more compelling lesson—that is—the critical importance of what goes on in what I will call the "risk" marketplace to average Americans.

Their savings—their pensions—their children's education—in short—their financial futures are now as never before in play in this marketplace.

This GAO report is fine as far as it goes. But it leaves out the most important lesson, in my view.

And that is: The vital role played by state securities regulators. We need more cops on the securities beat—and more constructive competition among them—to protect the investing public.

A regulatory monopoly is as bad as any other kind of monopoly. Customers and investors are ill-served by monopolies.

Monopoly regulators, like monopoly companies, get complacent. They miss things. They can get too cozy with the folks they're supposed to regulate. I've seen how it works in the securities industry. The regulators and the regulated go to each others conferences, usually in nice places like Palm Beach and Palm Desert.

The revolving door through which federal regulators go to find lucrative jobs on Wall Street should be the subject of another hearing on another day.

As I said, we probably wouldn't be here today if the SEC had done its job.

Unfortunately it did not.

From my perspective, as a state securities regulator, I think the SEC has to be aggressive across the board. Chairman William Donaldson made some important progress during his time at the Commission.

The pending nomination of Mr. Cox and other anticipated vacancies at the SEC raises a most serious question—is the era of reform and vigorous enforcement over?

There is no doubt we are at a crossroad. Just two years ago the House of Representatives voted by a margin of 418 in favor to 2 against to reform the mutual fund industry. The bill died in the Senate. Was that just for show?—or are we serious about giving average Americans real protection.

Over the years, the SEC has been criticized for not being proactive and tough enough. I think it's a fair criticism.

Traditionally, one of the weakest and most toothless divisions at the SEC was Investment Management. It has not been known for aggressive examinations, and certainly not for enforcement actions. I'd even call it a regulatory backwater.

This is strange—and unacceptable—given that nearly 100 million Americans entrust their money to the mutual fund industry.

Yet here we have a regulator that ignored reports from academics and even anonymous tipsters from within the industry that market timing was costing investors billions of dollars.

This chicanery and fraud would likely still be going on if it weren't for a couple of state securities divisions that acted when the SEC and NASD did not, despite having a tiny fraction of the resources these two organizations have.

In Massachusetts, for example, we brought several market-timing and late-trading enforcement actions based on tips we received and exams we conducted. These involved Putnam Mutual Funds, Prudential Securities, Franklin-Templeton and A.G. Edwards.

Like state securities regulators across the country, we follow up on tips. We answer the phone. We listen to investors. We're easy to reach.

There are those who would like to see state securities regulators just go away. They argue that our complementary system of state, federal and industry self-regulation is burdensome and duplicative.

It is neither. Quite the contrary. It serves to protect investors. The mutual fund trading abuses described in this GAO report are proof of that.

Our system works. That's the lesson of all this.

So next time some free-market think tank, underwritten by Wall Street money, says we don't need state securities regulators, that the industry can regulate itself just fine out of enlightened self-interest—you have a simple four-word answer, which also happens to be title of this report: "Mutual Fund Trading Abuses."

The fact is, we need more, not fewer, cops on the securities beat. That is the lesson of this scandal.

And we need cooperation among regulators, not co-option. We need to check each other's work sometimes. We need to backstop each other.

Years ago, in the name of so-called regulatory reform and efficiency, the states were essentially pre-empted from the regulation of mutual funds. The scandal we are here today to discuss is a legacy of that misguided policy.

Investor protection—including aggressive enforcement of state and federal securities laws—isn't a partisan issue.

Democrats, Republicans, Libertarians, Greens and Independents—they all rely on our nation's securities markets for their financial futures.

Investors vote and they're a very large constituency—larger than teachers, larger than labor, bigger than the AARP and bigger than the Baby Boomers.

They need to be protected. They're relying on us. If for some reason investors lost faith in our markets, it would be more than a pocket-book issue. It would be a national security issue.

We can't allow that to happen.

To sum up, the lessons of this sad chapter in Wall Street's history are simple: While the SEC and the NASD dropped the ball, the states picked it up. The system worked.

Now we are about to write the next chapter—will it be back to business as usual?—or will it be real protections for the hard-earned money that our citizens have invested.

The answer is up to us.

Thank you, Mr. Chairman.

Mr. CANNON. I couldn't help but think while you were talking about the incomparable Andrew Jackson and his veto of the Second National Bank's charter, which was passed by a Congress populated by a large number of people on the payroll of the Second National Bank. And in America, the reason we are having this hearing is because we need to strive to break up those cozy and often funded relationships that result in a loss of confidence. The only way you can have confidence is by having transparency and by having what you call protection; that is, enforcement against those people who commit crimes. And I love your idea. Pardon me for taking a couple of moments here, but I love the idea of cooperation and competition among enforcement agencies.

Thank you very much, Mr. Galvin.

And Mr. Zitzewitz.

TESTIMONY OF ERIC W. ZITZEWITZ, STANFORD GRADUATE SCHOOL OF BUSINESS, STANFORD, CALIFORNIA

Mr. ZITZEWITZ. Chairman Cannon, Ranking Member Watt, and Members of the Committee, thank you for the opportunity to appear here today.

We are discussing two recent reports by the GAO that ask whether there are lessons to be learned from the SEC's handling of recent issues in the pricing and trading of mutual fund shares. Both reports deal with the general issue of regulatory capture, whether the SEC is influenced by the industry in a way that adversely affects investors, and whether reforms can make it more immune to that influence.

The first report concluded that the SEC was aware of inefficiencies in the pricing of mutual fund shares that created arbitrage opportunities, and that it relied too heavily on assurances from the industry that they were preventing these inefficiencies from being exploited. This was despite being aware of evidence to the contrary: academic studies of the issues, press reports, complaints from investors and fund employees, and the high fund share turnover rate publicly reported by some international mutual funds.

The GAO report focuses on failings in the handling of referrals and in routine inspections. It does not mention policymaking, and I understand there are some jurisdictional issues involved, but that's an issue to which I will return.

The second report examines the negotiation of settlements with fund advisors who priced their funds in a way that created arbitrage opportunities and then facilitated arbitrage trading. The report appeared motivated by concerns that prosecutorial discretion could lead to excessive leniency, leniency that might be rewarded in a staff member's post-SEC career.

The GAO concluded that participation in the settlement negotiations was broad, and that negotiations were always conducted in the context of a damage analysis by SEC economists, and that this limited the influence of any individual. That said, the GAO concluded, and the SEC concurred, that improved monitoring of the subsequent employment of SEC enforcement staff would be a useful reform.

Before commenting on these two issues, I should preface everything by noting that the SEC and mutual fund industry have made a remarkable amount of progress in addressing these issues since September of '03. Furthermore, while economists often critique the incentives created by and the outcomes of an institution's design, we do so without impugning the character and work of its staff. I have met many members of the SEC in the last 2 years, and without exception found them to be smart and dedicated people whose primary concern is that our capital markets operate as efficiently and fairly as possible. Nothing I say today should be taken to imply otherwise.

The GAO reports are very thorough, and they adroitly handle a set of very sensitive issues. My only major critique of the first report is that it reflects the conventional framing of the market timing issue as one of trading abuses as opposed to one of pricing inefficiencies. The difference is subtle, but important for two reasons. First, focusing on pricing rather than trading leads one to the correct policy fixes. And second, focusing on pricing leads one to ask the right or at the very minimum an additional set of questions about the pre-2003 SEC stance on this issue.

The great irony is that the SEC understood the inefficiencies in international mutual fund pricing and had twice urged the industry to eliminate them through a procedure known as fair value pricing. But when the industry resisted, the SEC essentially backed down, despite the fact that it was clear from publicly available data that most funds were fair valuing infrequently if at all. The SEC provided no further formal guidance on this issue.

Even since September 2003 there has been in some cases a striking similarity between what the industry's asked for and what the SEC has proposed. The primary direct fix for the market timing problem proposed by the Investment Company Institute in October of '03 was a mandatory 2 percent fee for redemptions within 5 days of purchase. As I and others pointed out at the time, a severe limitation of this fix is that arbitragers could just hold their shares until day 6. Even if enforcement of the rule were perfect, it would only reduce the excess return available to the arbitragers by a factor of roughly 2. Despite this limitation this exact proposal became the primary direct fix for the market timing problem proposed by the SEC.

What I and others argued at the time would be a better first step is for the SEC to set and enforce standards for fund valuation that would substantially eliminate any arbitrage opportunity. Doing so would largely eliminate the need for measures such as monitoring and short-term trading fees. It will also eliminate the component of arbitrage that these measures will never be able to address.

While the industry has made progress in improving the valuation of international equity funds, there is still scope for further improvement. In other asset classes, such as illiquid bonds and small cap equity, substantial arbitrage opportunities still exist. This is possible because the industry is waiting for guidance on evaluating these asset classes from the SEC. There have been rumors for some time that the SEC is planning to issue such guidance, but there appears to be a delay. Regardless, the question remains why fixing the valuation of funds is the last step being taken as opposed to the first.

This brings me to my only substantial critique of the second report, which is also about the report's scope more than its content. The second report focuses on one form of regulatory capture while neglecting one potentially more important. The report is concerned with firm-level capture where a prosecutor might settle on attractive terms with a fund advisor and then go work for that advisor. My suspicion is that this scenario is fairly unlikely, particularly in the current climate. A more likely and difficult-to-address form of capture is industry-level capture in which a prosecutor settles on attractive terms out of fear that aggressive prosecution of a member of the industry will limit his or her subsequent career throughout the industry, or alternatively in which a policymaker is reluctant to push a policy that an entire industry opposes for the same reason. Is this type of capture a problem? The experience with pre-'03 policymaking suggests that it might be, while the scale of the penalties summarized in the second GAO report suggest that it's not.

The important question, of course, is not about what happened in the past, but what we can expect in the future. The extent to which the changed regulatory environment in '03-'04 turns out to be temporary or permanent, of course, remains to be seen.

How does one address this form of capture? The economists' answer would be higher salaries and longer employment tenures at the SEC to reduce the importance of post-SEC income. Personally I am a little more optimistic about my guess as to what the sociologists' answer would be: to collectively recognize that capture is a problem and that attempting to influence policy in this manner as opposed to winning arguments based on the facts is not something that should be rewarded.

A more radical suggestion would be to revisit the organization of SEC. Currently the policymaking divisions of the SEC are largely organized around the industries they regulate. A well-known empirical regularity is that single industry regulators are typically more prone to capture than mutli-industry regulators. The reason is straightforward. A DOJ lawyer prosecuting a case against the vitamin cartel need not seek future employment from the vitamin industry, whereas this is less true for an airline pricing specialist at the CAB seeking to limit a requested airfare increase. In this sense the current organization of the SEC may be exacerbating the influence of industry. If a formal reorganization is viewed as too costly, then a positive step may be to simply institutionalize the cross-functional involvement that the second GAO report notes was a favorable feature of the SEC's work on fund settlements.

In conclusion, thank you for the opportunity to share with you my thoughts on these issues. I look forward to your questions.

Mr. CANNON. Thank you, Mr. Zitzewitz.

[The prepared statement of Mr. Zitzewitz follows:]

PREPARED STATEMENT OF ERIC W. ZITZEWITZ

Chairman Cannon, Ranking Member Watt, and Members of the Committee, thank you for the opportunity to appear here today.[1] We are discussing two recent reports by the Government Accountability Office (GAO) that ask whether there are lessons to be learned from the Securities and Exchange Commission's (SEC) handling of recent issues in the pricing and trading of mutual fund shares.[2] Both reports deal with the general issue of regulatory capture – whether the SEC is influenced by the industry in a way that adversely affects investors and whether reforms can make it more immune to that influence.

The first report concluded that the SEC was aware of inefficiencies in the pricing of mutual fund shares that created arbitrage opportunities, and that it relied too heavily on assurances from the industry that they were preventing these inefficiencies from being exploited.[3] This was despite being aware of evidence to the contrary: academic studies of the issue,[4] press reports,[5] complaints from investors and fund employees, and the high

---

[1] I should begin by disclosing that in the last four years I have consulted, sometimes for compensation, with state and federal regulators, mutual fund families, two industry associations, law and consulting firms, and a pricing vendor. University rules limit my consulting to 20 percent of my time and I generally try to keep it to about 10 percent, so most of these engagements have been very short-term in nature.

[2] The reports are GAO-05-313, "Mutual Fund Trading Abuses: Lessons Can Be Learned from SEC Not Having Detected Violations at an Earlier Stage," and GAO-05-385, "Mutual Fund Trading Abuses: SEC Consistently Applied Procedures in Setting Penalties, but Could Strengthen Certain Internal Controls."

[3] For an example of such an assurance, see the 12/4/1997 speech of then Director of the Division of Investment Management Barry Barbash to the Investment Company Institute: "Funds that determined not to use fair value pricing at all or only in limited circumstances in October gave various reasons for their decisions. Some noted that fair value pricing can involve complicated judgment calls that are susceptible to second-guessing. Others pointed out that fair value pricing takes more time and is more costly to implement than pricing by reference to market quotations. Moreover, these funds asserted, the possibility of significant dilution in the value of their shares was not high enough to warrant the additional costs of fair value pricing." (http://www.sec.gov/news/speech/speecharchive/1997/spch199.txt). This reliance on industry assurances is also reflected in some of the early press reports on this issue. See, for example, "Monitoring Trades for the Good of the Shareholders," *New York Times*, 4/9/2000 and "Frequent Trading Worries Fund Firms," *Wall Street Journal*, 9/22/2000, C1.

[4] Academic work on mutual fund pricing inefficiencies includes Bhargava, Rahul, Ann Bose, and David Dubofsky, 1998, "Exploiting International Stock Market Correlations with Open-End Mutual Funds," *Journal of Business, Finance, and Accounting*, 765-773; Chalmers, John, Roger Edelen, and Gregory Kadlec, 2001, "On the Perils of Security Pricing by Financial Intermediaries: the Wildcard Option in Transacting Mutual-Fund Shares," *Journal of Finance*, 2209-36; Goetzmann, William, Zoran Ivkovic, and Geert Rouwenhorst, 2001, "Day Trading International Mutual Funds: Evidence and Policy Solutions," *Journal of Financial and Quantitative Analysis*, 287-309; Greene, Jason and Charles Hodges, 2002, "The Dilution Impact of Daily Fund Flows on Open-End Mutual Funds," *Journal of Financial Economics*, 131-158; Boudoukh, Jacob, Matthew Richardson, Marti Subrahmanyam, and Robert Whitelaw, 2002, "Stale Prices and Strategies for Trading Mutual Funds," *Financial Analysts Journal*, 53-71; and Zitzewitz, Eric, 2003, "Who Cares About Shareholders? Arbitrage-proofing Mutual Funds," *Journal of Law, Economics,*

fund share turnover rates publicly reported by some international mutual funds.[6] The GAO report focuses on failings in the handling of referrals (by the Division of Enforcement) and in routine inspections (by the Office of Compliance Inspections and Examinations). It does not mention policy making (by the Division of Investment Management), an issue to which I will return.

The second report examines the negotiation of settlements with fund advisors who priced their funds in a way that created arbitrage opportunities and then either facilitated or, in some cases, engaged in, arbitrage trading. The report appeared motivated by concerns that prosecutorial discretion could lead to excessive leniency, leniency that might be rewarded in a staff member's post-SEC career. The GAO concluded that participation in the settlement negotiations was broad and that negotiations were always conducted in the context of a damage analysis by SEC economists, and that this limited the influence of any individual. That said, the GAO concluded, and the SEC concurred, that improved monitoring of the subsequent employment of SEC Enforcement staff would be a useful reform.

Before commenting on these two issues, I should preface everything by noting that the SEC and mutual fund industry have made a remarkable amount of progress in addressing these issues since September 2003.[7] Furthermore, while economists often critique the incentives created by and outcomes of an institution's design, we do so without impugning the character or work of its staff. I have met many members of the

---

and Organization, 245-280. Goetzmann, Ivkovic, and Rouwenhorst (2001), Greene and Hodges (2002), and Zitzewitz (2003) also included evidence on the extent of arbitrage trading, and Boudoukh, Richardson, Subrahmanyam, and Whitelaw (2002) discussed the existence of stale price arbitrage hedge funds.

[5] See, for example, Gavin, Daly, "In Lean Times, Firms Reconsider Timers," *Ignites.com*, 4/19/2002, Stone, Amey, "When Market Timers Target Funds," *Business Week Online*, 12/11/2002, and Carnahan, Ira "Looting Mutual Funds," *Forbes.com*, 3/19/2003.

[6] In contrast, there is no evidence I am aware of that the SEC was aware of the extent or even the existence of late trading in mutual funds.

[7] Specifically, as of the fourth quarter of 2004, the average international fund was removing about 70 percent of the price staleness in its NAVs via fair value pricing; up from about 7 percent in 2002. Dilution due to stale price arbitrage trading has been reduced to less than 5 basis points in international equity funds (at least in the TrimTabs sample of funds). Furthermore, I can no longer find evidence of late trading, at least in the fund-level data that I have access to. At the same time, valuation issues remain in other asset classes, particularly fixed income, and there is some (weak) evidence that arbitrage in high yield bond funds is increasing. See "Update on the Pricing and Dilution of Mutual Funds" (available at http://faculty-gsb.stanford.edu/zitzewitz/Research/mfupdate.pdf) for details.

SEC staff in the last two years, and without exception have found them to be smart and dedicated people whose primary concern is that our capital markets operate as efficiently and fairly as possible. Nothing I say today should be taken to imply otherwise.

The GAO reports are very thorough, and they adroitly handle a set of very sensitive issues. My only major critique of the first report is that it reflects the conventional framing of the "market timing" issue as one of "trading abuses" as opposed to one of pricing inefficiencies.[8] The difference is subtle, but important for two reasons. First, focusing on pricing rather than trading leads one to the correct policy fixes.[9] And second, focusing on pricing leads one to ask the right (or, at minimum, an additional set of) questions about the pre-2003 SEC stance on this issue.

The great irony is that the SEC understood the inefficiencies in international mutual fund pricing[10] and had twice urged the industry to eliminate them through a procedure known as fair value pricing.[11] But when the industry resisted, the SEC essentially backed down.[12] Despite the fact that it was clear from publicly available data that most funds were fair valuing infrequently, if at all, the SEC provided no further formal guidance on the issue.[13]

---

[8] Late trading, of course, is clearly a trading abuse, not a pricing problem, and can only be dealt with through restrictions on post-4 p.m. trading.

[9] For reasons I discuss in Zitzewitz (2003), attempting to combat NAV arbitrage via trading restrictions or redemption fees suffers from both limited effectiveness and the fact that they selectively applied (or not applied) to certain investors. Simply put, if you are known to be in the habit of predictably mispricing financial assets, lots of people are going to want to trade with you – the key is to eliminate the mispricing to the extent possible.

[10] A 1981 no-action letter to Putnam discussed these issues, suggesting that SEC understanding of them issues dates at least to 1981.

[11] I am referring to the letters of 12/8/1999 and 4/30/2001 from Douglas Scheidt of the SEC to Craig Tyle of the Investment Company Institute (available at http://www.sec.gov/divisions/investment/guidance/tyle120899.htm and http://www.sec.gov/divisions/investment/guidance/tyle043001.htm).

[12] See, for example, a 2001 letter to the SEC from the Bar Association of New York and a 2002 white paper by the Investment Company Institute (cited and quoted from in Zitzewitz, 2003). It is worth noting that since this time period, there has been a complete turnover in the top management of the ICI.

[13] Surveys of valuation practices by Deloitte and Touche, PriceWaterhouseCoopers, and Capital Market Risk Advisors also revealed that many fund firms were either not fair valuing or using extremely wide thresholds. See also Sahoo, Alison, "Fund Firms Lagging When It Comes to Valuation," *Ignites.com*, 10/18/2001 and Sahoo, Alison, "Funds Still Not Up to Snuff on Valuation." *Ignites.com*, 11/19/2001. I did hear in early 2003 that the SEC was placing more emphasis on fair value in its compliance visits to funds,

Even since September 2003, there has been in some cases a striking similarity between what the industry has asked for and what the SEC has proposed.[14] The primary direct fix for the market timing problem proposed by the Investment Company Institute in October 2003 was a mandatory 2% fee for redemptions within 5 days of purchase. As I and others pointed out at the time, a severe limitation of this fix is that arbitrageurs could just hold their shares until day 6; even if enforcement of the rule were perfect, it would only reduce the excess returns available to arbitrageurs by a factor of roughly 2 (i.e., from about 48% per year to 24%, assuming no accompanying increase in fair value pricing).[15] Despite this limitation, this exact proposal became the primary direct fix for the market timing problem proposed by the SEC.

What I and others argued at the time would be a better first step is for the SEC to set and enforce standards for fund valuation that would substantially eliminate any arbitrage opportunity.[16] Doing so would largely eliminate the need for measures such as monitoring and short-term-trading fees, it will also eliminate the component of arbitrage that these measures will never be able to address.[17] While the industry has made progress in improving the valuation of international equity funds, there is still scope for further improvement. In other asset classes, such as illiquid bonds and small-cap equity, substantial arbitrage opportunities still exist. This is possibly because the industry is waiting for guidance on these asset classes from the SEC. There have been rumors for some time that the SEC is planning to issue such guidance, but there appears to be a

---

and my analysis of the public NAV data reveals a slight increase in its use in early 2003 (see "Update on the Pricing and Dilution of Mutual Funds").

[14] Of course, in other cases, the SEC has proposed and approved rules that the industry opposed, such as the requirement that fund trustee board chairpersons be independent.

[15] See my 11/6/2003 testimony to the House Committee on Financial Services, Subcommittee on Capital Markets, Insurance, and Government-Sponsored Enterprises (available at http://financialservices.house.gov/media/pdf/110603cz.pdf).

[16] See, for example, the academics quoted in "A Band-Aid for the Fund Industry's Broken Leg?" *New York Times*, 11/21/2003, 1. It is likely impossible to completely eliminate all predictability from mutual fund NAVs, but we can come a lot closer to doing so than we do currently.

[17] For example, an arbitrageur in a stale-priced international fund can earn abnormal returns of 5 percent of year even while always observing holding periods of at least 90 days. Even longer-term shareholders with a knowledge of the details of mutual fund pricing can make their purchases and sales on days when pricing inefficiencies are in their favor.

delay. Regardless, the question remains why fixing the valuation of funds is the last step being taken, as opposed to the first.

This brings me to my only substantial critique of the second report, which is also about the report's scope more than its content.[18] The second report focuses on one form of regulatory capture, while neglecting one potentially more important. The report is concerned with firm-level capture, where a prosecutor might settle on attractive terms with a specific fund advisor, and then go work for that advisor (or, as the report does not consider directly but perhaps should, for a professional services firm that serves that advisor). My suspicion is that this scenario is fairly unlikely, particularly in the current climate.

A more likely, and difficult to address, form of capture is industry-level capture, in which a prosecutor settles on attractive terms out of fear that aggressive prosecution of a member of the industry will limit his or her subsequent career throughout the industry. Or, alternatively, in which a policy maker is reluctant to push a policy that an entire industry opposes, for the same reason.

Is this type of capture a problem? The experience with pre-2003 policy making suggests that it might be, while the scale of the penalties summarized in the second GAO report suggest that it is not.[19] The important question, of course, is not about what happened in the past, but what we can expect in the future. The extent to which the changed regulatory environment in 2003-4 turns out to temporary or permanent remains to be seen.

---

[18] To the extent that the scope was given in advance, my comments are not really critiques so much as suggestions for future work.

[19] One caveat: while the GAO compares the size of the penalties to those in previous enforcement actions, an additional relevant comparison would be to the magnitude of shareholder dilution in each case. In Canada, the Ontario Securities Commission made public its estimate of shareholder dilution when each settlement was announced (it was generally about twice the settlement figure). It would seem reasonable to ask that the SEC do the same. Note that doing so would presumably not influence the outcome of any private litigation, since the litigants are very likely to obtain this information, if they have not already. It would, however, inform the public's evaluation of the fairness of the settlement process.

How does one address this form of capture? The economist's answer would be higher salaries and longer employment tenures at the SEC, to reduce the importance of post-SEC income. Personally, I am a little more optimistic about my guess as to what the sociologist's answer would be: to collectively recognize that capture is a problem and that attempting to influence policy in this manner, as opposed to winning arguments based on facts, is not something that should be rewarded.

A more radical suggestion would be to revisit the organization of the SEC. Currently, the policy-making divisions of the SEC (Corporation Finance, Investment Management, Market Regulation) are largely organized around the industries they regulate. A well-known empirical regularity is that single-industry regulators are typically more prone to capture than multi-industry regulators. The reason is straightforward: a DOJ lawyer prosecuting a case against a vitamin cartel need not seek future employment in the vitamin industry, whereas this is less true for an airline pricing specialist at the Civil Aeronautics Board seeking to limit a requested airfare increase. In this sense, the current organization of the SEC may be exacerbating the influence of industry. If a formal reorganization is viewed as too costly, then a positive step may be to simply institutionalize the cross-functional involvement that the second GAO report notes was a favorable feature of the SEC's work on fund settlements.

In conclusion, thank you again for the opportunity to share with you my thoughts on these issues. I look forward to your questions.

Mr. CANNON. Does the gentleman from North Carolina seek recognition?

Mr. WATT. Thank you, Mr. Chairman.

Mr. CANNON. The gentleman's recognized for 5 minutes.

Mr. WATT. Ms. Richards, I am trying to assess whether there is a different attitude at the SEC regarding oversight and enforcement related to mutual funds than there is at the SEC regarding other securities. First of all, is there a different attitude, and if so, why? Second, is there a different level of personnel numbers quality, and if so, why? You said there were 500 employees overseeing the mutual funds. What would be the comparable number, for example, overseeing other kinds of securities matters? Could you just talk about that a little bit to see whether there is some historic difference in attitude?

Ms. RICHARDS. Sure. Let me say at the outset, my office examines stock exchanges, broker-dealers, transfer agents, as well as mutual funds and investment advisors. I was a member of the SEC's enforcement division for 10 years before I came to this job. Our examiners are uniformly, I believe, aggressive, and they are incentivized to find problems. The mission of the SEC is to detect fraud. Having examiners in a single division, I think, allows us to be single-minded and focused in that goal. Similarly, having enforcement staff in a single division, with their only goal is to prosecute violations of the securities law, I think helps further that mission.

I can speak very candidly and personally about the attitude of my staff certainly in the exam program, but also of the SEC staff, that our mission and our goal is to detect fraud. Chairman Donaldson, when he came to the SEC, his primary goal in terms of managing the SEC was to institute reforms that would allow us to see around the corner and over the hill to detect the next type of emerging fraud and to be better focused on emerging risks in the securities industry.

Mr. WATT. I'm not sure I have yet heard, is there a division with reference to mutual funds enforcement and other securities enforcement, or is it all one?

Ms. RICHARDS. It's all in one. The examination function for all those entities in the securities industry is in one program. The enforcement function is in one program. There are other offices of the SEC that do policymaking. Within the examination program we have now about 500 staff people who are responsible for examining mutual funds and investment advisors. We have about 350 staff people who examine broker-dealers. They are complemented by the work of the stock exchanges. The self-regulatory organizations also have examiners that examine broker-dealers. With respect to the stock exchanges, we have about 50 staff people who are responsible for examining the stock exchanges.

Mr. WATT. So you actually have more people on mutual funds because there are other supervisory entities such as the stock exchanges' broker-dealer associations that are self-governing. Is there not a separate self-governing entity for mutual funds?

Ms. RICHARDS. That's right. The mutual funds have no self-regulatory organization, so the SEC is the primary regulator, complemented certainly by the work of other regulators, including

State securities regulators, but there is no equivalent in the mutual fund industry, no equivalent self-regulatory organization.

Mr. WATT. Mr. Zitzewitz, what say you about this issue that I addressed to her, and how might it be improved?

Mr. ZITZEWITZ. Sir, when I was referring to the organization of the SEC, I was referring primarily to the policymaking divisions. I think that having a single division for enforcement and a single division for inspections makes a lot of sense. I suppose within those divisions for expertise reasons it's always going to make sense to have some people focusing on one area and some people focusing on another area.

I think, though, it's useful to consider the fact that there might be a trade-off between allowing employees to build expertise and having it be the case that once they have done that, their future employment has to come from that industry. It may be that having large numbers of specialists might make sense to temper that with some cross-functional specialization if you're thinking about controlling sources of potential capture.

Mr. WATT. Thank you, Mr. Chairman. I yield back.

Mr. CANNON. I thank the Ranking Member.

The Chair would announce that it's his intention to allow the other Members here to ask questions before I ask questions. So the Chair recognizes Mr. Delahunt for 5 minutes.

Mr. DELAHUNT. Thank you, Mr. Chairman.

I would be interested in the opinion of both Ms. Richards and Secretary Galvin about the relationship between Federal and State regulators. I have a concern. You might have heard the banter up here earlier, about there's never too much oversight. And Mr. Galvin expressed it as in terms of there's not enough cops on the beat.

Now, I don't know what happened, you know, prior to September of 2003, but clearly there were abuses that either were not identified or were identified and were not pursued by the SEC. I'm not interested in the history. I'm interested in solving the problem. But having been a State prosecutor myself, I know that oftentimes there are problems in relationships between State agencies and Federal agencies. But to use the military concept of a force multiplier, where do we stand in terms of the relationship between the State regulators and the SEC at this point in time? And let me begin with Ms. Richards, and then I would ask Secretary Galvin.

Ms. RICHARDS. Well, I agree with everything you just said. There are vast numbers of securities firms. We are outmanned and outgunned by the securities firms that we regulate. There are compliance departments of some of the large securities firms that outnumber SEC in terms of the number of exam staff that we have. To me that means that it's terribly important that we work together with our colleagues at the State level. And in my program, in the examination program, we have a history of doing just that.

We meet with our colleagues across the country in regular examination planning summits to plan priorities, to plan targeted initiatives, to plan joint work and joint training. I believe it's terribly important that we leverage off of one another. We're made much more effective when we're all working together.

There are certainly times where there are differences of opinion. I suppose in any relationship that's bound to happen. I think, speaking personally, it's terribly important that we not let those differences of opinion overcome the need for us to work together.

Mr. DELAHUNT. Let me interrupt you, and I will pose that same question to Secretary Galvin.

Mr. GALVIN. Thank you. I think you have to understand one thing especially with regard to mutual funds that has to be said. Ms. Richards has already mentioned the vast number of mutual funds that we have and the difficulties that that presents in any kind of enforcement regulation. But there's also a bigger problem, it seems to me, and that is that mutual funds have—the regulation of mutual funds has not really kept pace with the role they play in our investment savings system. You know, we still treat mutual funds in many respects like it was some sort of a small group of people sitting around a table trying to decide how to invest like a stock club. They have become the bank of necessity for most Americans. Most Americans have found themselves, whether directly or indirectly, invested in mutual funds out of a sense of safety perhaps, or indirectly through their employer or some other means.

So the challenge presented by mutual funds is greater perhaps than many of the other segments of the securities industry.

As far as the cooperation, I think cooperation is improved. I think the experiences of 2003 have helped that. I—at the same time, I think there are some distinctions that have to be drawn. Generally speaking, the State securities regulators, of course, are operating with people in their respective States, individual consumers, more likely to hear about smaller problems, individual problems, than perhaps industry-wide problems.

I think the States accept the fact, as we ought to, that the second should be the primary policymaker when it comes to market-wide policies. There's no question about that.

When it comes to enforcement, I do think a little bit of competition is healthy. We have never failed to refer something to the SEC, at least in Massachusetts, when we thought it was appropriate. We also have, in fact, referred them to Federal prosecutors and State prosecutors when we thought it was appropriate. I do think cooperation is improving.

I think the other player in this whole discussion, though, which has to be brought to the table or at least mentioned, is the attitude of the industry itself, which has resisted any kind of regulation and indeed has been the sponsor many times of efforts at State preemption. That clearly is out there and——

Mr. DELAHUNT. I mean, we have to deal with the issue of preemption, not just in terms of this particular issue, but the whole array of issues that come before this Committee. The Ranking Member is the Chair of the States Rights Caucus. He is not here right now. I have assumed the title of vice president. One would be shocked at the number of bills that come out of this Committee that preempt State law.

If the Chair would indulge me for an additional minute.

Mr. CANNON. Without objection.

Mr. DELAHUNT. Yes. I just want to pursue, I guess, with both of you, but in terms of the jurisdiction of this particular Subcommittee which falls in the area of compliance and enforcement, is there any legislation?

Let me direct this to you, Mr. Secretary, and you can respond, Ms. Richards, what you feel would add, if you will, to that cooperation, which I think is absolutely essential.

You know, all too often, people can be going down the same roads not being aware of what is happening in a parallel universe, so to speak. I would be more than willing to consider working with you and with others to file that legislation, because I think you are both right. That industry is a very, very powerful industry in terms of resources.

I don't think, Ms. Richards, you have the resources necessary. I know that at the State level they face the same fiscal constraints.

Mr. GALVIN. If I may, and one thing I may have referred to in my testimony is, I think it was a mistake in the 1996 act to limit the States' authority of mutual funds. There were amendments made to section 18 of the 1933 act, and I think that was a mistake.

Now, if there needs to be some better definition of the relationship, that's fine. But simply to say that the States are limited to fraud when they see it or when they hear about it, I don't think was the right way to go.

I think—again reflecting the unique situation of mutual funds, I don't think it's an exaggeration to say that most small savings banks around the country are under a greater degree of scrutiny on their day-to-day operations than mutual funds, despite the fact that they hold many more billions, trillions of dollars.

And I think the one thing that there is absolutely no disagreement among Federal and State regulators about is the inadequacy of us, collectively even, to try to deal with this.

Mr. DELAHUNT. How do we solve that problem, Ms. Richards——

Mr. GALVIN. Well, we certainly don't want to crimp—we certainly don't want to crimp the free market. And mutual funds have done a great deal for people in this country. But I think we have to make sure that our regulatory efforts and our enforcement effort is up to par to meet the challenge presented by the vast number of them. So that's what I am saying.

I think, looking at some of the changes made in 1990 and 1996—you are asking in terms of specific legislation—would be one thing. There may be other remedies which, I don't know whether they would jurisdictionally be before this Committee or other Committees.

But one of the things that troubles me when I look at the whole industry is the whole issue of mandatory arbitration of disputes and the way that the panels are set up that make those decisions. Investors are forced into agreeing to an arbitration process that I believe—and it is my personal opinion—is stacked against them.

If we are going to say—and we all agree we don't want them in the courts. We don't want them in the courts. They don't belong in the courts,but nevertheless, there'd better be a safer system and a better system for people to get relief when they need it.

That may be another area that you might want to look at.

Mr. DELAHUNT. Mr. Chairman, that suggestion, I am confident, is within the jurisdiction of this particular Subcommittee.

Mr. CANNON. The gentleman yields back. Thank you.

The gentlelady from Florida is recognized for 5 minutes.

Ms. WASSERMAN SCHULTZ. Thank you, Mr. Chairman. And I am truly looking forward to serving on this Committee, hopefully, as of tomorrow. And I appreciate the accommodation that you and the Ranking Member have given me today.

I, too, sit on the Financial Services Committee as my other Committee assignment, so we have spent a little bit of time on this issue in that Committee.

Just to piggyback on what the gentleman from Massachusetts asked you, Ms. Richards and Secretary Galvin and, actually, anyone who chooses to answer it—not so much how you can, what legislation you would need or how the law would need to be changed for better coordination between State and Federal regulators, but my question is, do you feel you need any change in the law, generally, to do a better job of regulating?

Ms. RICHARDS. I guess I would demur on the question of whether the SEC would seek legislation. I would ask for permission to come back to you with that.

The SEC has taken, as I said, a number of rule-making initiatives, using its own authority to better shore up the internal governance, the internal controls, and the compliance operations of mutual funds. For the first time, beginning last October, all mutual fund firms are required to have a chief compliance officer and written policies and procedures for the first time.

I think that that is one of the most significant steps the SEC has taken in terms of ensuring better compliance by mutual funds themselves.

We then, as the GAO report notes, are responsible for making sure that those chief compliance officers are really doing their job; and if they are really doing their job in detecting and deterring violations of the law, I think we are all—we are all better served by that.

In terms of—in terms of coordination, there are a number of ongoing initiatives between the SEC and the State regulators. And the picture is not as bleak as Secretary Galvin would maybe paint it. We have regular examination planning summits, regular meetings about enforcement topics. We worked very effectively with the State securities regulators, not only with respect to market timing and late trading, but before that with respect to analysts' conflicts of interest.

Those relationships, I think, grow and develop over time. And I think they are terribly important at a SEC regional office level and a State level that we ensure that we grow and improve those relationships on the ground.

Ms. WASSERMAN SCHULTZ. Mr. Secretary.

Mr. GALVIN. Well, as I mentioned earlier, I think in terms of legislation, there needs to be—and I would suggest that you might look at the act that passed in late 2003, for some issues that were raised there. Some of them have been addressed by rule-making, and I applaud the SEC for that. I do say there has been an improvement in the coordination. I know definitely in our, for instance, region in Massachusetts, there has been an improvement in cooperation; and I am pleased for that.

But I do think, again it gets back to understanding the vastness of the mutual fund industry. There is a definite attitude problem persisting in that industry, in my opinion, and I think there needs to be sufficient address of these issues, such as, how do we remedy problems that individual investors have, sales practices—which I know Ms. Richards referred to in her testimony, and I agree with her. It is a very important area; it is continuing to be a problem, I think.

As we look at some of the relationships that funds have with suppliers of funds, as they treat their customers context, other interaction with other individual customers, what they offer them as a—the role of pension funds and how individual investors find themselves caught up with a particular fund, either by a company or union or whoever directs them in that way—the relationships of those that direct that business to the mutual funds have with the pension funds. Those are all issues that I think are appropriate for enforcement and review and perhaps for regulation.

Ms. WASSERMAN SCHULTZ. The other issue that was fairly disturbing in my review of the problems that are going on now: Chairman Donaldson has obviously done an excellent job at taking some fairly aggressive steps in getting a handle on it, but it was pretty disturbing to learn that there really haven't been any post-employment restrictions, the revolving door back and forth between SEC employees, former employees, going into the mutual fund industry, the industry that they had formerly regulated. And I just wonder what steps are being taken, because that was pretty disturbing.

Ms. RICHARDS. Thank you for asking me that question. SEC examiners are absolutely prohibited from discussing employment during an ongoing examination. They are absolutely prohibited from doing that. There are obvious conflicts of interest in that process.

We are making our process more formal. Once an examination has concluded and the examiner has determined to discuss employment outside the SEC with a firm that we regulate and has made a determination to go to that firm, the employee must, as part of a formal exit procedure, notify the supervisor where they intend to go to work. That supervisor will then conduct a thorough review of conflicts of interest, including asking, Did you, as an examiner, ever participate in an examination of that firm? This process is a more formal process than we have in place now.

We certainly agree with the GAO that we can shore up our conflicts of interest procedures to make sure that there is no question that SEC examiners are acting without conflicts of interest or the appearance of a conflict of interest.

Ms. WASSERMAN SCHULTZ. Thank you, Mr. Chairman.

Mr. CANNON. The gentlelady's time has expired.

Without objection, the record will be kept open for 5 legislative days for follow-up questions to the witnesses.

Without hearing objection, so ordered.

Now, I am deeply intrigued by the fact that many of the issues we are dealing with today are not really partisan issues, they are issues of how we solve fundamental problems. I suppose you could make them partisan, but I think one of the things we hear today is an inquiry of where we ought to go as opposed to any partisan divide.

I was deeply intrigued, Mr. Secretary, by your idea of needing more cops and more competition in enforcement and tying that to cosy relationships.

You know, we all hope that people don't get co-opted, but they actually do. And so the idea of having multiple agencies that see different things, hear different things, have different relationships with their citizens, seems to be really interesting.

I was just asking the staff up here—we don't think there is an interstate compact dealing with securities enforcement. Are you aware, Mr. Secretary?

Mr. GALVIN. No, there is not a compact. We do have an association. Regulation at the State level varies in where it resides. In 12 States, it resides in the office I hold, secretary of state, or the equivalent thereof. In a very few States, it resides with the attorney general's office. In many States, it resides in the executive agency of the State and in some places corporate commissions.

But there is an umbrella organization that we have of State securities administrators that is helpful as an exchange of information and to present our point of view, and also effectively, I think, to give our point of view to the SEC. But there is no individual compact.

Cooperation among States, however, is high. In general, when matters occur in one State that appear to have roots in another, there is frequent communication between the States and among the States.

Mr. CANNON. The jurisdiction of this Committee is over interstate compacts. In my earlier days, I worked in the Interior Department with the Office of Service Mining back in the very early days of the regulation of the coal mining industry and the reclamation process. And we ended up devolving regulatory authority to the States, and it worked remarkably well.

As a matter of fact, I was handed a "60 Minutes" investigation when I walked in the door. And by the time it got to television it was actually an exoneration of the Reagan administration, which I thought was actually fairly remarkable.

So over a long period of time, a person could become committed to the idea that we do a much better job, and that was the conclusion about the Office of Service Mining; that is, at the Federal level is very difficult to do the kind of regulation that you could do in the States.

In that case, you had a geographic distribution. But here it seems to me that you also have a great deal of opportunity to improve the way you enforce and bring more resources to the enforcement if you organize and are given a Federal charter to do an interstate compact.

Is that a matter of interest, do you think?

Mr. GALVIN. It is interesting. I think we have to explore further exactly what we mean.

But I definitely think as we go forward—and I note your comments, and I appreciate them about the bipartisan nature of the problem and about the future, because that is really what it is about. But I think, as we go forward, one of the things we will all confront is that, increasingly, for most people in the country their financial future is going to be more in the risk marketplace.

Defined benefit pensions, I know in another part of the Capitol today there are hearings on those. Problems—we all know they are there—increase, and the individuals are going to find themselves navigating their own way through the marketplace.

So therefore I think some means of communication amongst the States, some plans, some protocols, are certainly helpful.

Now, there are different philosophies amongst the States; I must say that there are—as is to be expected.

Mr. CANNON. It is a competitive market. That's what we want actually.

Mr. GALVIN. That's good. That's good. But I still think there are certain base things. I mean, fraud is fraud and misrepresentation is misrepresentation. So I think there is some benefit to looking into that.

As I said, I think there is no question the SEC must be the primary rule maker for national policy. Must be. But on an enforcement basis on some of the problems that emerge and some of the new techniques, this is a very inventive industry, the securities industry. Many of us—we could collectively agree as regulators we could solve this problem, and indeed we may well have, but they will find a new way to do it.

So they are very creative. So I think we have to be, as Ms. Richards was quoted as saying, over the hill, looking over the hill. And so I think perhaps more people looking at it on a State level might be a good thing.

Mr. CANNON. Could I ask your insight on one other item?

In my personal life I invested in what they call the Thrift Savings Plan, TSP. Here, locally, we have four options; and we have, I suspect—I have never actually followed up on this, but the group that actually looks at the performance of those funds, which means that both the SEC and the States have an additional reach—in other words, you have got a bunch of cops who are looking at that on behalf of me and the many other thousands of public employees, Federal employees, that invest.

Is there a way that we can empower more people to get involved in funds or more fund managers who can coordinate with your activities at the State and Federal level—this is both for Ms. Richards and Mr. Galvin—so that we can increase the security of individual investors by having a private layer of people who watch funds?

Mr. GALVIN. Well, I think that it's touching a very important area and a growing area of concern, namely, the intermediaries that have control over directing individual employees' fund investments.

Not long ago I was invited to speak to an audience of local public pension managers in Massachusetts, and during the course of my remarks—in fact, it was during lunch; they were eating while I was speaking, which was all right with me. But during the course of the lunch, I went on to talk in a very tangential way about some of the problems with people taking free things from people they were investing with—free golf, free this, free that. Deadening silence.

I don't mean to suggest that they were all acknowledging some sort of misdeed, but I think it comes as a revelation to some of these folks, who are actually not professional investors—they might be just other employees or union leaders, something like that, that are empowered with this responsibility—that they really have to exercise a fiduciary duty.

And that is really the fundamental part, whether we are talking about mutual fund management, or even pension management or whatever it is, the responsibility of getting the best deal you can for the people you are representing.

So I think—in this area that you are referring to, I think that the States certainly could provide some additional benefit—many of these smaller investors are in more limited plans—not just the places that manage them, but perhaps where the decisions are made in an individual State. This is certainly an area where I think the States could be of assistance because of the vastness of the problem.

Ms. RICHARDS. I think, Mr. Chairman, your question is very timely. Just 2 weeks ago the SEC released the results of an examination sweep of pension consultants. These are investment advisors who are relied on to be the experts to help pension plan administrators navigate amongst the many intermediaries out there trying to sell them services.

What we found in those examinations was that about half of the pension consultants also received money from the mutual funds or the investment advisors that they also may have been recommending to the pension plans. These, we thought, were serious conflicts of interest which needed to be addressed by pension consultants.

So I think your question is timely and right on point with some of the work that we have been doing in our risk-based examinations.

Mr. CANNON. Thank you.

Mr. WATT. Could the Chairman yield for just a sec?

Mr. CANNON. Certainly.

Mr. WATT. Is what you just described illegal?

Ms. RICHARDS. Yes. Existing law under the Federal securities laws requires these firms to disclose material conflicts of interest.

One of the most disturbing findings——

Mr. WATT. But is it illegal after they disclose it? I mean, can you take action against them?

Ms. RICHARDS. If they don't disclose these conflicts of interest, yes, sir.

Mr. WATT. No, that's not what I asked. I asked, is it illegal if they disclose it? Is it illegal? Can you take action against them?

Ms. RICHARDS. No, sir. If they were disclosing it, it would be legal. What we found, however, was that they were not disclosing these conflicts of interest.

Mr. WATT. And what is the penalty for nondisclosure?

Ms. RICHARDS. We referred many of these firms to our Division of Enforcement, who is looking at these nondisclosures.

We also made our findings public so that pension consultants, not just the firms we examined—there are 1,700 firms in this business—could look at our findings and make changes to make sure that they were disclosing these conflicts of interest.

We think this is——

Mr. WATT. I guess the question I am asking is, does this Congress need to be making the law a brighter line standard or increasing the penalties? What do we need to be doing to help you all?

I mean, you said you were outmanned, outgunned. Is it more personnel? Is it more staff? Is it a more enforceable law? What is it that we need to do?

Ms. RICHARDS. I am not—I am not sure that it would be presumptuous of me to come to you with recommendations for this legislation. I think the securities laws adequately address this problem that I have just talked about.

I think one of the things we are very much focused on at the SEC is using the resources we have in a more efficient, more productive and more nimble way.

Mr. CANNON. The gentleman yields back.

My time having expired, let me thank the panel for being here.

Mr. DELAHUNT. Could I just ask a few follow-up——

Mr. CANNON. Very insightful. Would you like to be recognized?

Mr. DELAHUNT. Yes, please.

Mr. CANNON. The gentleman is recognized.

Mr. DELAHUNT. Again, I want to concur with the sentiment you expressed. But I guess I am frustrated because, in summary, where the law seems to be adequate here, how come we missed so much up until 21 months ago? As you said, Chairman Donaldson is talking about looking around the horizon and around the curve.

If we don't somehow better coordinate, you know, between the States and the Federal Government—do you have like a shared data base, and do we have—as a former prosecutor that conducted a lot of white-collar investigations in conjunction with U.S. Attorney's office and other Federal investigative agencies, we had a protocol which allowed for cross-designation. We had our own arrangement to do referrals, if you will. There was a constant sharing of information.

Does that exist?

Ms. RICHARDS. One of the findings of the GAO report is that with respect to market timing and late trading, we coordinated effectively with our colleagues at the State level, including with criminal prosecutors; and criminal prosecution of the Federal securities laws is a terribly important complement to what we do on the civil side.

Mr. DELAHUNT. But that was missing up until 21 months ago. I mean, I just perused the GAO report, and one of the issues seems to be a lack of a consistent policy in terms of referral.

Ms. RICHARDS. No, I think what the GAO found—and I won't speak for Mr. Hillman—is that we could better document our referrals to criminal authorities, but the relationships, if you will, are ongoing and are informal and are active.

Mr. DELAHUNT. See, my problem is informal. I have no doubt that you are an outstanding professional. And I concur with the good professor there in terms of the quality of people that are on the staff. But that changes, that waxes and wanes like anything.

I guess I am looking for some sort of—whether it's in the form of legislation, some other—maybe it's by a compact of some sort among the States, whether it's a formal mechanism, where this information moves around. Because there is no way that you are combined that—independently, that you have, even probably when you combine your resources—you can take on the kind of tasks that are an order of magnitude that clearly are enormous.

You know, Secretary Galvin is right. You know, the era of the defined benefit, that is gone. We are not going to see pensions, you know, like my parents and others enjoyed in the 1950's and 1960's. People are going to be left to their own navigating the mutual fund industry and the securities industry just to survive.

I mean, we are talking about Social Security reform. You know, that's the end, if that happens, you know, that's the end of the defined benefit plan.

But, again, I guess my frustration is, I want to know, and I think the American people have a right to know, that there is some sort of formal mechanism that requires an information-sharing and resource-sharing between the States and the Federal Government.

Ms. RICHARDS. Yes, sir.

In 1997, the SEC signed a memorandum of understanding with the Association of State Securities Administrators (ASSA),[1] that requires that we meet at least once a year on the national level and discuss emerging types of fraud, and more frequently on the local level.

Mr. DELAHUNT. Good. You know, having a summit once a year—I have been at a lot of summits, okay, and a lot of conferences. But I am talking about requiring, you know, agencies—and make it a 2-way street that this becomes automatic on the—required and mandated by statute, as opposed to informal relationships that are obviously very important.

Ms. RICHARDS. Yes, sir.

Mr. DELAHUNT. However, that changes once, you know, Richards and Galvin are gone and Professor Eric and Hillman—I mean, then we have a whole new slate and maybe those relationships aren't the same.

Mr. CANNON. If the gentleman would yield, let me point out, this is a complex environment you are talking about. It would take a great deal to put together, but I would suspect that it makes an enormous amount of sense.

I don't want to interrupt you, Ms. Richards, you obviously had an answer. But I frankly think this is an interesting place to go.

Ms. RICHARDS. I was just going to echo what you said, that this agreement between the SEC and the State securities regulators has been in place since 1997. And the whole purpose of it was to mandate these kinds of regular meetings, regardless of changes in staffing at the State or Federal level.

There are regional examination planning summits that take place, I believe it is twice each year; and Secretary Galvin could talk about those, because I am sure he has participated in those along with our staff in the Boston office.

But the whole goal was to make sure that there is that kind of mandated meeting and sharing of information and strategy planning about how we can use our resources.

---

[1] The memorandum of understanding was actually signed with the North American Securities Administrators Association (NASAA).

Mr. DELAHUNT. Right, and I am sure that is very positive. And I am sure the Secretary and the other panelists would agree.

But I guess what I am saying is, I want more than an MOU, okay? I mean, I am coming from a different angle. Because I know, when I was the district attorney up in the metropolitan Boston area, I had MOUs. I had no idea whether my successor has, in those agencies that we had memoranda of understanding with, you know, complied with it today. You know, it's probably gone the way of—of——

Mr. WATT. Of Bill Delahunt.

Mr. DELAHUNT.—of Bill Delahunt, exactly.

Mr. CANNON. The gentleman yields back.

Again, let me thank the members of the panel and the Committee for your time. And we stand adjourned.

[Whereupon, at 5:26 p.m., the Subcommittee was adjourned.]

APPENDIX

Material Submitted for the Hearing Record

Prepared Statement of the Honorable Chris Cannon, a Representative in Congress from the State of Utah, and Chairman, Subcommittee on Commercial and Administrative Law

In the fall of 2003, the New York State Attorney announced what would become the first of many law enforcement initiatives that his office, other state officials, and the SEC would later champion to ferret out mutual fund trading abuses. Within the ensuing months, many well-respected mutual fund companies and others were caught up in this scandal, including Canary Capital, Janus Capital Group, Bank of America, Alliance Capital Management, Prudential Securities, Millennium Partners, Fred Alger Management, Putnam Investments, Massachusetts Financial Services, Security Trust, Franklin Resources, and Invesco Funds Group.

In the fall and winter of 2003, it seemed as if every day the press reported on yet another shocking instance of mutual fund trading abuses. These abuses included the illegal practice of late trading, which involves trading shares after the markets have closed so that the trader can take advantage of information that becomes available after the closing. The Congressional Research Service analogized this practice to "a racetrack that allows certain customers to bet on yesterday's races."

Other abuses included the more nuanced problem of market timing. Market timing typically involves frequent buying and selling of mutual fund shares by sophisticated investors, such as hedge funds, that seek opportunities to make profits on the differences between foreign and domestic markets.

While not per se illegal, market timing can constitute illegal conduct if, for example, it takes place as a result of undisclosed agreements between investment advisers and favored customers in contravention of stated fund trading limits. Frequent trading can harm mutual fund shareholders because it lowers fund returns and increases transaction costs.

According to an estimate prepared by one of the witnesses at today's hearing, Professor Zitzewitz, market timing abuses may have resulted in $5 billion in annual losses. As of November 2003, the SEC estimated that 50 percent of the 80 largest mutual fund companies had entered into undisclosed arrangements permitting certain shareholders to engage in market timing practices that were inconsistent with the funds' policies, prospectus disclosures, or fiduciary obligations.

As the mutual fund scandal unfolded, questions were raised about the fitness of the SEC's overall regulation, inspection, and enforcement of this industry. The Congressional Research Service posed possible explanations, including the following:

- The possibility that SEC's resources devoted to the fund industry were dwarfed by the expansion in the number of mutual funds.
- The possibility that the SEC's overall effectiveness may have been marred by inter-divisional disharmonies.
- The possibility that SEC officials may have placed too much trust in the fund industry's integrity and ability to police itself.
- The possibility that the mutual fund industry may be "too close" to the relevant parts of the SEC entrusted with its oversight and regulation.
- The possibility that the SEC may have had a somewhat understandable focus on the prevention of more traditional types of fund misconduct.

In response to these concerns, House Judiciary Committee Chairman Sensenbrenner and Ranking Member Conyers requested the GAO to undertake a comprehensive review of the SEC's efforts to proactively detect and prevent illegal activities in the mutual fund industry.

Today's hearing provides an opportunity for the GAO to report on its findings and recommendations and to allow the SEC and others to respond to them.

RESPONSE TO POST-HEARING QUESTIONS FROM LORI A. RICHARDS, DIRECTOR, OFFICE OF COMPLIANCE INSPECTIONS AND EXAMINATIONS, U.S. SECURITIES AND EXCHANGE COMMISSION

RESPONSES TO SUBCOMMITTEE MEMBERS' QUESTIONS POSED FOLLOWING THE JUNE 7, 2005 HEARING CONCERNING "*MUTUAL FUND TRADING ABUSES*"

U.S. HOUSE JUDICIARY COMMITTEE SUBCOMMITTEE ON COMMERCIAL AND ADMINISTRATIVE LAW

Responses to the following questions are provided by the staff of the Securities and Exchange Commission, including staff in the Office of Compliance Inspections and Examinations, the Division of Enforcement and the Division of Investment Management.

1. In light of the Supreme Court's recent decision overturning the obstruction of justice conviction of the Arthur Andersen accounting firm for destroying documents pertaining to Enron Corporation's finances, does the criminal law need to be clarified with regard to how document destruction would constitute the crime of obstruction of justice? (Division of Enforcement)

Arthur Andersen was prosecuted by the Department of Justice under 18 U.S.C. Section 1512 (b), which provides in relevant part that:

> Whoever knowingly uses intimidation, threatens, or corruptly persuades another person, or attempts to do so, or engages in misleading conduct toward another person, with intent to . . .
>
> (B) alter, destroy, mutilate, or conceal an object with intent to impair the object's integrity or availability for use in an official proceeding; . .
>
> shall be fined under this title or imprisoned not more than ten years, or both.

The Supreme Court vacated Arthur Andersen's conviction because of an erroneous jury instruction which did not convey the statute's requisite consciousness of wrongdoing. Specifically, the jury was instructed that "even if [Arthur Andersen] honestly and sincerely believed that its conduct was lawful, you may find [it] guilty." The jury instruction also stated that the jury could find Arthur Andersen guilty if the firm intended to "subvert, undermine, or impede" governmental fact-finding by suggesting to its employees that they enforce the firm's document retention policy. The Supreme Court found that the instruction did not include a key element of the statute, the element of consciousness of wrongdoing required by the words "knowingly" and "corruptly."

Statutes and regulations enacted subsequent to Arthur Anderson's indictment pursuant to the authority of the Sarbanes-Oxley Act ("SOX") imposed provisions of the law regarding an auditor's requirement to retain audit records and work papers. These provisions are described below.

Section 1519 of Title 18, which was added by SOX, addresses the destruction or alteration of documents in federal investigations and bankruptcies. It provides in relevant part:

> Whoever knowingly alters, destroys, mutilates, conceals, covers up, falsifies, or makes a false entry in any record, document, or tangible object with the intent to impede, obstruct, or influence the investigation or proper administration of any matter within the jurisdiction of any department or agency of the United States . . . shall be fined under this title, imprisoned not more than 20 years, or both.

Unlike the statute that Arthur Andersen was charged under, this statute does not contain an element of "corruptness."

Conversely, SOX also added Section 1512(c), which is directed towards an individual who "corruptly – alters, destroys, mutilates, or conceals a record, document, or other object, or attempts to do so, with the intent to impair the object's integrity or availability for use in an official proceeding; ..." Again, unlike the statute at issue in the Arthur Andersen prosecution, it does not contain an element of "knowingly."

Furthermore, SOX also enacted Section 1520 of Title 18 entitled "*Destruction of Corporate Audit Records.*" Section (a)(1) requires that auditors maintain all audit or review work papers for a period of 5 years from the end of the fiscal period in which the audit or review concluded. Section (a)(2) authorized the SEC to promulgate rules and regulations relating to the retention of broad categories of audit documents. Consistent with that delegation of authority, the SEC amended Regulation S-X by adding 17 C.F.R. Section 210.2-06, addressing the retention of audit and review records ("*Retention of Records Relevant to Audits and Reviews.*" Release Nos. 33-8180, 34-47241, and IC-25911 (January 24, 2003), available at www.sec.gov/rules/final/33-8180.htm). This regulation, effective on March 3, 2003, requires that audit and review documentation be retained for 7 years. Knowing and willful violations of this regulation are punishable by a fine, imprisonment for not more than 10 years, or both.

Finally, the Public Company Accounting Oversight Board ("PCAOB") was required by Section 103(a)(2)(A)(i) of SOX to adopt an auditing standard that required accounting firms registered with it to retain a broad category of audit and review papers for a period of time not less than 7 years. Consistent with this directive, the PCAOB included a requirement that such documents be maintained for 7 years (Auditing Standard No. 3, "Audit Documentation," para.14). This standard is enforceable by both the PCAOB and the SEC.

In sum, as a result of SOX, there now exist several additional legal provisions that require auditors to retain audit and work papers, and which could form the basis of a criminal prosecution in the event of similar conduct today. Given these provisions, the precise issue that led to the Supreme Court's decision to vacate Arthur Andersen's conviction is unlikely to arise again.

2. Would greater civil and/or criminal penalties better deter abuse? (Division of Enforcement)

With the Insider Trading Sanctions Act of 1984, the Securities Enforcement Remedies and Penny Stock Reform Act of 1990 ("Remedies Act"), and more recently, the Sarbanes-Oxley law,

Congress has provided the Commission with significant flexibility in determining when to impose a civil money penalty, and how much of a penalty to impose. In setting penalties, the Commission considers the Remedies Act's three-tier penalty guide and other core factors, such as the type of violation, degree of harm to investors, and whether the wrongdoer is a recidivist. This framework provides the Commission the flexibility it needs to tailor penalties to the seriousness of the wrongdoing. Determining the size of the money penalty is a vital step in achieving the desired deterrent effect under the securities laws, especially in light of the exponential growth of our capital markets in the past decade. The combination of strong enforcement of the law and the tailoring of significant and meaningful remedies such as money penalties, disgorgement and bars from the securities industry, all serve to better deter abuse.

A coordinated approach between the Commission and the criminal authorities also serves to deter abuse. The Commission strives to work closely with criminal authorities where appropriate, especially in the more egregious cases. In fact, the Commission coordinated with criminal authorities in 131 cases in FY 2003, and 159 cases in 2004.

3. Does the SEC encounter any difficulty in obtaining documents, such as emails, during its examinations? (Office of Compliance Inspections and Examinations)

To address this question it would be helpful to provide some background on the Commission's expectations on the production of electronic records. In 2001 the Commission proposed to require investment advisers to produce required records that are maintained in an electronic format within one business day of examiners' requests ("*Electronic Record Keeping by Investment Companies and Investment Advisers,*" Release Nos. IC-24890 and IA-1932 (March 13, 2001) 66 Fed. Reg. 15369, 15373 (March 19, 2001)), available at www.sec.gov/rules/proposed/ic-24890.htm. Ultimately, however, the Commission decided not to adopt this approach. Instead, the Commission required advisers to provide such reports "promptly." The Commission said:

> We are not adopting a proposed amendment that would have stated that records are to be provided in no case more than one business day after a request. Some commenters were concerned that such an amendment could preclude funds and advisers from reaching an accommodation with the examination staff to produce certain documents immediately and other documents that are not immediately accessible, on a delayed basis. We agree that such arrangements when entered into and performed in good faith by funds or advisers can facilitate the examination process. While the "promptly" standard imposes no specific time limit, we expect that a fund or adviser would be permitted to delay furnishing electronically stored records for more than 24 hours only in unusual circumstances. At the same time, we believe that in many cases funds and advisers could, and therefore will be required to, furnish records immediately or within a few hours of request. ("*Electronic Recordkeeping by Investment Companies and Investment Advisers,*" Release Nos. IC-24991 and IA-1945 (May 24, 2001)(adopting Rule 204-2(g)(2)(ii) under the Investment Advisers Act) 66 Fed. Reg. 29224, 29225 (May 30, 2001), available at www.sec.gov/rules/final/ic-24991.htm.

The Commission has made similar statements with respect to broker-dealer's production of records during examinations. Much like the production of adviser records, broker-dealers' must furnish their records "promptly" upon request. Rule 17a-4(j). When the Commission adopted this standard, it indicated that it expected "promptly" to mean "almost immediately" ("*Broker-Dealer Recordkeeping and Preservation Requirements,*" Release No. 34-19190 (October 29, 1982)). Specifically, the Commission said: "In many, if not most, instances the rule generally will require the broker-dealer to turn over copies of the required records almost immediately. The time to turn over the records will, however, in all cases, depend on the particular circumstances" *Id.* at n. 4.

To implement the Commission's stated expectations, examiners generally expect that firms will provide electronic communications almost immediately, and that they will not furnish electronic records for more than 24 hours "only in unusual circumstances." Nonetheless, in particular circumstances, such as where the records are not immediately accessible, examiners may agree to longer production schedules. These agreements often lead to "rolling productions" in which electronic communications are produced to examiners according to an agreed-upon schedule. A rolling production schedule also allows the firm time to have counsel review selected emails for possible claims of attorney-client privilege. In most cases, examiners and the firm are able to devise an appropriate and timely schedule for the production of emails.

While most examinations proceed in an reasonable and timely fashion, unfortunately, some firms seek to delay unreasonably or otherwise interfere with the production of electronic records. Examiners are alert to any indication that a production is being made in less than good faith. In addition, the Commission has taken enforcement actions against firms and individuals that:

- destroyed emails instead of producing them to the staff; *see In the Matter of Schield Management Company and Marshall L. Schield,* Initial Decision Release No. 284 (May 24, 2005)(ALJ decision in adjudicated administrative proceeding), available at www.sec.gov/litigation/aljdec/id284bpm.htm.

- failed to produce emails to the staff in a timely manner; *see In the Matter of Strong Capital Management, Inc., Strong Investor Services, Inc., Strong Investments, Inc., Richard S. Strong, Thomas A. Hooker, Jr. and Anthony J. D'Amato*, Release Nos. 34-49741, IA-2239, and IC-26448 (May 20, 2004), available at www.sec.gov/litigation/admin/34-49741.htm., and

- misled the staff about the availability of emails requested by the staff; *see In the Matter of Banc of America Securities LLC,* Release Nos. 34-49386 (March 10, 2004), available at www.sec.gov/litigation/admin/34-49386.htm.

4. Besides market timing and late trading, are there other mutual fund trading abuses that have come to light, for example, instances of brokers receiving undisclosed payments for steering investors toward specific funds? (Office of Compliance Inspections and Examinations)

In 2003, the SEC began to focus its examination resources on the activities and firms that pose the greatest risk to investors. Our goal was to develop a more anticipatory approach, in which we would focus on emerging or resurgent forms of fraudulent, illegal or questionable activities. Risk-targeted examination reviews are a reasonable and effective means of quickly addressing risks in the securities industry. The benefit of risk-targeted reviews in promptly identifying emerging trends and compliance problems has already been demonstrated. For example, as a result of coordinated reviews of both mutual funds and the broker-dealers that distribute their shares, we found that fund assets were increasingly being used to pay broker-dealers for "shelf space" and that disclosure of these practices was sometimes poor or non-existent. The SEC brought several enforcement actions, adopted new rules restricting funds' ability to use brokerage for distribution and is considering improved "point of sale" disclosure to customers. *See, e.g. In the Matter of Edward D. Jones & Co., L.P.*, Release Nos. 33-8520 and 34-50910(December 22, 2004), available at www.sec.gov.litigation/admin/33-8520.htm, *In the Matter of Franklin Advisers, Inc. and Franklin/Templeton Distributors, Inc.*, Release Nos. 34-50841, IA-2337, and IC-26692(December 13, 2004) available at www.sec.gov/litigation/admin/34-50841, *"Prohibition on the Use of Brokerage Commissions to Finance Distribution,"* Release No. IC-26591(September 2, 2004) available at www.sec.gov/rules/final/ic-26591.htm, and *"Point of Sale Disclosure Requirements and Confirmation Requirements for Transactions in Mutual Funds, College Savings Plans, and Certain Other Securities, and Amendments to the Registration Forms for Mutual Funds,"* Release Nos. 33-8544, 34-51274, IC-26778 (February 28, 2004) available at available at www.sec.gov/rules/proposed/33-8544.htm. In another example, we recently completed a risk-targeted review of pension plan consultants. We found significant conflicts of interest and inadequate disclosure of those conflicts and released a public report describing what we found. *See "Staff Report Concerning Examinations of Select Pension Consultants,"* (May 16, 2005), available at www.sec.gov/news/studies/pensionexamstudy.pdf. In both of these situations, and in others, our examinations have revealed significant compliance problems involving mutual funds and advisers.

5. Widespread mutual fund trading violations were first detected and acted on by state regulators, not the SEC. Why did the SEC miss these trading abuses and what steps has it taken to better detect and deter them? Can you provide assurance that these abuses are now under control? (Office of Compliance Inspections and Examinations)

In 2003, following a tip, the New York Attorney General began investigating market timing abuses by several market participants. Shortly thereafter, Commission examiners and enforcement staff began a large-scale investigation which revealed the size and extent of the problem in the industry. Prior to 2003, the Commission staff did not identify indications of the secret arrangements that some market timers had with some mutual funds. These arrangements were collusive, non-disclosed agreements allowing the market timer to engage in trading that deviated from the fund's policies and procedures or disclosed policy with respect to the frequency of trading, and were often evidenced in e-mail communications. Prior to 2003, SEC examinations of mutual funds were focused on activities that appeared to pose the greatest risk of compliance problems – in particular, activities that might be designed to overstate the fund's returns or subject investors' money in the fund to undisclosed risk. This approach was based on the fact that fund portfolio managers generally attempt to attract investors by producing strong returns. Examination protocols focused on portfolio management, order execution, allocation of investment opportunities, pricing, and calculation of net asset value. Examinations focused on the fund itself, and not on trading in the fund's shares.

The SEC has enhanced its program for examining mutual funds. Changes include: the development and use of risk based examinations; reviewing e-mails during examinations; more frequent examinations of higher risk firms; a surveillance program under consideration for funds and advisers; and other program changes (described in more detail in the testimony of Lori A. Richards, before the Subcommittee on Commercial and Administrative Law on June 7, 2005).

Importantly, the SEC has significantly enhanced the governance of investment companies and strengthened their compliance abilities by adopting some new rules. In the wake of the mutual fund enforcement actions involving late trading, market timing, and the misuse of nonpublic information about fund portfolios, the Commission determined that many of these failings could be attributed to a serious breakdown of management controls. Recognizing that the fund boards, and especially independent directors on fund boards, are responsible for overseeing all operations of the fund, the SEC adopted new fund governance rules that were designed to give more authority to directors that are independent of the funds management teams. *See, "Investment Company Governance,"* Release No. IC-26520 (July 27, 2004), available at www.sec.gov/rules/final/ic-26520.htm.

As a compliment to the governance rule, the SEC adopted a rule that requires investment companies and investment advisers to have written compliance policies and procedures reasonably designed to prevent violations of the federal securities laws. These policies must be reviewed annually for their effectiveness and the firms must designate a chief compliance officer who reports directly to the fund board. The rule fosters a strong compliance culture that is essential to institute and enforce a strong system of controls that prevent securities laws violations and protect the interests of shareholders and clients. The authority of fund boards to control management and fund operations is strengthened when the chief compliance officer reports directly to the fund board. *See, "Compliance Programs of Investment Companies and Investment Advisers,"* Release Nos. IA-2204 and IC-26299 (December 17, 2003), available at www.sec.gov/rules/final/ia-2204.htm.

6. In one instance, the SEC received a tip that market timing abuses were occurring at one fund company, yet the SEC did not act on it. Instead, the tipster went to a state regulator, who subsequently opened an investigation. What steps has the SEC taken to improve its tip-handling process? (Division of Enforcement)

The SEC staff received information concerning market timing by fund customers in early 2003, reviewed the information, and concluded that there were no indications of violations of the federal securities laws. Several months later, SEC staff received a *separate* tip involving different information – that the fund insiders were themselves market timing the fund. The SEC rapidly investigated this conduct and in October 2003 filed an enforcement action against the fund firm involving abusive trading by insiders.

The SEC receives thousands of complaints and tips each year, and views these communications as a very valuable source of information and leads with respect to violative conduct. The SEC has adopted procedures designed to ensure stringent review and oversight of the way fraud-related complaints to the Enforcement Division are handled. These procedures for handling complaints, tips, and referrals apply to all enforcement staff and require staff receiving complaints, tips or referrals regarding potential illicit conduct to confer with supervisors about appropriate handling, respond to complainants, and add information about the complaint and the complainant, including the actual or recommended disposition of the complaint or tip, to a dedicated database. Senior Enforcement staff review the database periodically. To date, more than 3,600 investor complaints are documented in the agency's growing database.

7. While the penalties the SEC has obtained in the mutual fund trading abuse settlements are generally higher than what the SEC has obtained in past settlements, the investment advisers involved included some of the most prominent and wealthiest in the industry. Does the SEC consider these penalties high enough to provide effective deterrence? What, if anything, precludes SEC from seeking higher penalties? (Division of Enforcement)

We believe that the totality of the remedies obtained in the market timing/late trading cases send a compelling and effective message of deterrence. In total, the Commission has obtained orders for more that $2.2 billion in these cases. Money penalties are an important component in the package of remedies that serve to deter future violations of the securities laws. Once the Commission determines that it is appropriate to seek a money penalty, it strives to tailor the size of the penalty to the seriousness of the violations. In addition to determining the size of the penalties, the Commission carefully considers the appropriateness of imposing other significant remedies, such as disgorgement and undertakings. The totality of the remedies obtained in a case, and the specter of reputational damage, send a compelling message of deterrence to the parties in the case, as well as other potential wrongdoers in the industry.

The current statutory framework provides the Commission with strong tools with which to seek tailored and appropriate penalties in enforcement actions that warrant penalties. The Commission's authority to determine whether to impose a penalty and to set the amount of a penalty is in Section 21(b)(3)(A) of the Exchange Act, Section 203(h) of the Investment Advisers Act, and Section 9(d) of the Investment Company Act. The Commission has the ability to seek and impose penalties in administrative proceedings against entities and persons directly regulated by the Commission, such as broker-dealers or investment advisers, or in federal court actions against any entity or person. In determining the maximum amounts for penalties, these sections provide standards for setting first tier (non-fraud), second tier (fraud), and third tier (fraud plus substantial losses or significant risk thereof) penalties.

In district court actions the Commission may impose penalties up to the greater of either the defendant's pecuniary gain resulting from violation or an amount within the three-tier framework. In accordance with the Debt Collection Improvement Act of 1996, the Commission has adopted rules that adjust for inflation the maximum amount of the penalties set forth in the statutes. Currently, for both district court and administrative proceedings, the three tiers of penalties and maximum penalties for each tier are: $6500 for a natural person and $65,000 for any other person for first tier penalties; 65,000 for a natural person and $325,000 for any other person for second tier penalties; or $130,000 for a natural person and $650,000 for any other person for third tier penalties. The maximum penalty may be assessed "for each violation" (in a district court action) or "for each act or omission" giving rise to the penalty (in an administrative proceeding). An important step in determining the size of the penalty is consideration of the number of "violations" or "acts or omissions" that have been committed by the wrongdoer. The statutory framework allows a significant degree of flexibility in determining what constitutes a "violation" or "acts or omissions," and as a result, a wide range of maximum penalties are available. In addition to considering the three statutory tiers, the Commission may further tailor the size of the penalty by considering factors such as the type of violation at issue, the harm that the conduct has caused to the public, and whether the wrongdoer is a recidivist.

8. Of the approximately $2 billion of penalties and disgorgement imposed for the market timing and late trading violations, how much has been collected? How much of this has been returned to investors? Could you describe how this was done for the mutual fund investors affected by the market timing and late trading violations? (Division of Enforcement)

Of the $2,130,813,151 ordered to be paid in penalties and disgorgement imposed for the market timing and late trading violations, $1,951,038,278 has been collected. The remaining balance of $180,079,347 to be paid in penalties and disgorgement is a result of payment plans established for the specific parties. For example, the final payment of $161,342,466 for *Invesco Fund Group, Inc.* is not due to be paid until December 31, 2005.

Monies Collected have not yet been returned to the investors. The primary goal of all Commission enforcement actions is to deter and penalize securities law violators, and thus the Commission continues to prosecute the entities and persons responsible for market timing and late trading violations. Now that money has been collected in the market timing and late trading cases, the Commission's enforcement staff is dividing its resources into prosecuting new cases and returning funds to defrauded investors, as further described below.

The Commission is committed to promptly and fairly distributing the monies it has collected in the mutual fund market timing and late trading cases to the harmed investors. To that end, the Commission generally uses the services of an Independent Distribution Consultant ("IDC") to formulate a distribution plan. The plans must address numerous complex issues including: how to measure the extent to which the funds were diluted and the shareholders harmed; how to account for monies recovered from third parties through which the market timers acted; how to treat investors who no longer hold the subject funds; the de minimis damages amount, if any, below which investors will not receive a distribution; tax considerations; and how to deal with omnibus accounts, which are accounts held by brokers in their names, rather than in the names of specific customers, through which the brokers transact business on behalf of all their customers.

The process for creating the distribution plans has entailed extensive coordination between the various IDCs, the Commission staff, and others to ensure that the plan is fair. To date, IDCs have not yet submitted final plans to the Commission for approval, however it is expected that most will do so by the end of 2005. Once the Commission determines that a plan is fair and reasonable, the responsible IDC will notify the affected investors of the settlements, the investors will have an opportunity to make claims, and the monies will be returned to the victims.

9. Many of the settlements with high-ranking individuals involved in the market timing abuses included industry bars – some life-time, and others for a few years. How are these bars enforced? (Division of Enforcement)

The federal securities laws authorize the Commission, in its administrative proceedings, to bar individuals from association with regulated entities, including broker-dealers, investment advisers and investment companies. An individual subject to a bar must obtain Commission consent *prior* to becoming associated with a regulated entity in any capacity prohibited by the bar. A bar is a permanent sanction, and even if an individual obtains consent to associate, that consent will apply only to employment by a specific employer in a specific capacity. The Commission often enters bar orders that contain a proviso that an individual may make application for consent to associate after a specified period of time. However, the bar does not expire at the end of that time, and the Commission may still exercise its discretion to deny consent if, for example, it finds that the individual has engaged in misconduct since imposition of the bar or that the proposed employer's supervision would be inadequate.

The federal securities laws make it unlawful, absent Commission consent, for a barred individual to associate with a regulated entity in violation of a bar, and for a securities industry firm to employ that individual in violation of the bar. A bar is also a "statutory disqualification" under the Securities Exchange Act that self-regulatory organizations must consider prior to allowing an individual to become or remain an associated person of a member firm. Violations of the bar may be remedied in federal court by seeking an injunction from further violations, or by seeking to convert the administrative order into a judicial order in civil proceedings pursuant to Section 21(e) of the Securities Exchange Act. In appropriate cases, the Commission may institute proceedings to impose additional administrative sanctions such as cease and desist orders or more stringent bars. (*See, e.g.*, *SEC v. Steven M. Bolla, et al.*, Litigation Release No. 18837 (Aug. 18, 2004) (injunction for violation of bar); *In the Matter of Steven M. Bolla, et. al.*, Securities Exchange Act Release No. 50222 (Aug. 20, 2004) (bar from association with any broker, dealer or investment adviser imposed for violation of earlier bar from association with any investment adviser that had contained proviso permitting application for consent to associate after five years); *In the Matter of Patrick J. Rooney and Adrian Antoniu Alexander*, Securities Exchange Act Release No 44414 (June 13, 2001) (cease and desist order issued for violation of bar orders; bars were also imposed upon the respondents to replace prior bars that contained a proviso permitting application for consent to associate after specified periods).

10. GAO recommends that the SEC begin documenting criminal referrals and the post-employment plans of departing staff. Why hasn't the SEC's criminal referral and exit process included these documentation procedures? What steps has the SEC taken to address GAO's recommendation? (Division of Enforcement and Office of Compliance Inspections and Examinations)

The process by which the SEC has referred most matters to criminal authorities has been informal, yet successful. We view criminal prosecutions as essential to providing appropriate deterrence in certain cases, and work with criminal authorities to effectively enforce the federal securities laws. In fiscal 2003, we brought 131 cases related to criminal proceedings; in 2004 we brought 159 such cases, and as of May 2005, 47 such cases. In the mutual fund market timing and late trading area, we coordinated extensively with criminal authorities. In fact, criminal authorities were aware of all Commission cases in that area. Of course, even highly effective processes can be improved.

GAO has recommended that we document informal referrals to the criminal authorities. We are converting our investigation opening form to a web-based application, which will provide for documentation of informal referrals to criminal authorities. By modifying the form, we will record the types of matters that are informally referred to criminal authorities and provide the reasons for the referral.

With respect to the post-employment plans of departing staff, the SEC provides training and guidance to its staff on federal laws and regulations regarding employment with regulated entities. We require former staff to notify the SEC if they plan to make an appearance before the agency, which includes dealing with SEC examiners. In the past, the SEC did not require departing staff to report where they planned to work. The SEC did not track post-employment information for several reasons. The agency's ethics training program made the staff aware of employment related restrictions. With respect to SEC examiners, they were and are prohibited from discussing employment with any firm during the pendency of an examination.

Nevertheless, the SEC has taken several additional steps to educate employees concerning post-employment restrictions and concerns regarding possible conflicts of interest. The SEC increased the number of ethics liaisons in the examination program, particularly in the field offices, developed enhanced training for ethics officials, and is planning more frequent training for all the exam staff. In addition, the SEC is developing a more formalized exit procedure for all departing staff that will include asking for the identity of their new employer, so line managers and others can follow-up on any conflicts with the employee's past work at the SEC.

11. Professor Zitzewitz suggests that a better first step for the SEC would be to set and enforce standards for fund valuation that would substantially eliminate any arbitrage opportunity. What is your response? (Division of Investment Management)

The Investment Company Act requires funds to calculate their net asset values using the market value of portfolio securities when market quotations are readily available. If a market quotation for a portfolio security is not readily available, or is unreliable, the fund must establish a "fair value" for that security, as determined in good faith by the fund's board. Fair value pricing can minimize market timing and eliminate dilution of shareholders interests. The Commission and its staff have articulated standards to be followed in fair value pricing in several settings, including: Accounting Series Release No. 118 (1970), and a letter to the Investment Company Institute (April 30, 2001). In addition, in the release adopting new compliance procedures for mutual funds, the Commission reiterated the obligation of funds to fair value their securities especially under certain circumstances to reduce market timing arbitrage opportunities. *See "Disclosure of Market Timing and Selective Disclosure of Portfolio Holdings,"* Release nos. 33-8408 and IC-26418, (May 28, 2004)(adopting release) available at www.sec.gov/rules/final/33-

8408.htm. Finally, the Commission has taken enforcement action against advisers that have engaged in improper pricing, *see, e.g. In the Matter of Garrett Van Wagoner and Van Wagoner Capital Management, Inc.*, Release Nos. IA-2281 and IC-26579 (August 26, 2004), available at www.sec.gov/litigation/admin/ia-2281.htm.

12. In his prepared statement, Professor Zitzewitz made the following statement:

> **[W]hile the GAO compares the size of the penalties to those in previous enforcement actions, an additional relevant comparison would be to the magnitude of shareholder dilution in each case. In Canada, the Ontario Securities Commission made public its estimate of shareholder dilution when each settlement was announced (it was generally about twice the settlement figure). It would seem reasonable to ask that the SEC do the same. Not that doing so would presumably not influence the outcome of any private litigation, since the litigants are very likely to obtain this information, if they have not already. It would, however, inform the public's evaluation of the fairness of the settlement process.**

What is your response to this statement? (Division of Enforcement)

In constructing a fair and appropriate settlement package, the securities laws afford the Commission the necessary flexibility to take a case-by-case view of the facts and circumstances of each case. The fairness and strength of a settlement also stems from consideration of the particular conduct at issue. In the market timing cases, the Commission considers shareholder dilution, in itself one measure of shareholder harm, a factor in the consideration of disgorgement. In addition to disgorgement, a meaningful settlement package typically includes, as appropriate, other remedies, such as penalties, undertakings and bars or suspensions from the securities industry. The Commission tends to refrain from identifying a single dilution figure in the public filings relating to the settlement of market timing cases, but rather focuses on the totality of the settlement package. Remedies such as the amount of penalties, disgorgement and the nature of other sanctions contained in settlement packages tend to lend themselves to relevant and reasonable comparisons of enforcement actions.

Consideration of the magnitude of shareholder dilution allows for a wide range of estimates of dilution to fund shareholders by abusive traders which may be available for the Commission's consideration at the time that a settlement is negotiated. This range is attributable to the many variables that may have an effect on the dollar value of particular estimates of dilution. Variables include the overall method of estimation employed, the time period used to encompass abusive trading that is subject to analysis, and the specific trades during that period that are analyzed. For example, one estimate may cover a year or two and another several years. In addition, one estimate may incorporate a very large set of analyzed trades within a given period of time and another estimate a smaller set of trades in the same period. In some cases, the settlement amount has equaled or exceeded estimates of dilution, in other cases it has not. In one case, *Alliance Capital Management,* the Commission's Order includes an express requirement that, if the measure of shareholder losses exceeds $200 million, Alliance is required to pay additional disgorgement to cover investor losses. In any event, most of the settlements require the respondents to retain consultants to formulate plans for distribution of the money to shareholders to compensate for losses. These distribution plans will be public and will reflect analyses of shareholder harm in that case. In sum, in light of the many variables at play in calculating shareholder harm, and in consideration of the importance of the totality of the settlement package, focus on one estimate of shareholder dilution may not necessarily lend itself to accurate and relevant comparisons in enforcement actions.

RESPONSE TO POST-HEARING QUESTIONS FROM THE HONORABLE WILLIAM FRANCIS GALVIN, SECRETARY OF THE COMMONWEALTH OF MASSACHUSETTS

MEMORANDUM

To: Susan Jensen
From: William F. Galvin, Secretary of the Commonwealth
Date: July 27, 2005
Re: Responses to Questions on Secretary Galvin's Testimony on June 7, 2005

1. How Did Massachusetts Determine that the Tip on Market Timing Abuses at Putnam Was Credible?

The Massachusetts Securities Division acted promptly to investigate a tip about trading abuses at the Boston-based Putnam mutual fund company.

The whistleblower in the Putnam case had the hallmarks of credibility; the information he provided was detailed and plausible. The whistleblower's job put him in a position to know the information he brought to us. Also, he was accompanied by an attorney who was experienced in securities issues. Moreover, the whistleblower specifically outlined how the fund Putnam's compliance procedures were being overridden or ignored. Based on this specific and credible information, the Securities Division promptly commenced a focused investigation.

The Massachusetts Securities Division acted immediately on this credible tip.

2. Cooperation Between the States and the SEC. Cooperation between the states and the SEC is improving both in the areas of mutual fund trading abuses and on the general oversight of the securities industry.

We believe that a diversity of regulators (state and federal) and a measure of competition among regulators in the area of enforcement is a healthy way to avoid the downsides of routine regulatory procedures and established decisions about policy implementation. The SEC's regulatory monopoly in areas relating to mutual funds allowed many problems to persist. The states were able to see that practices that had become established in many segments of the industry were abusive, and harmful to the interests of investors.

3. Do the Problems at the SEC Stem from a Lack of Resources or Staffing? The staffing and budget of the SEC have not kept pace with the explosive growth the financial industry and of mutual funds. Mutual fund investing is a pillar supporting many families' retirement and savings plans. The resources dedicated to the regulation of the mutual fund industry should reflect both the large scale of the industry and the fact that a majority of small investors and savers simply must do at least a portion of their investing and saving through mutual funds.

We cannot ignore the fact that the mutual fund industry is wealthy and powerful. In the recent past, the industry seems to be have been able to intimidate the SEC from taking strong regulatory initiatives. A related problem is that it is possible for regulators to become too close to the industry they are supposed to regulate –the revolving door phenomenon of former regulators going to work for the industry contributes to this problem.

In the instance of market timing trading abuses, the SEC had taken the view that market timing was probably a rare problem, and a problem that would be self limiting, since market timing trades would hurt fund performance. In practice, market timing abuses were widespread. Many fund companies used market timing practices as a way to increase the amount of assets under management, thereby increasing management fees for fund sponsors.

4. Interstate Compact.

Massachusetts is interested in exploring means by which the states can best coordinate fraud investigations and enforcement actions, which will result in better investor protection. An interstate compact may be a way to accomplish that.

Massachusetts is prepared to ask the North American Securities Administrators Association ("NASAA") to examine the value of having the states enter into a compact for the implementation and enforcement of their securities laws. We note that the creation of a compact relating to securities law among a large number of the states will involve issues of state administrative law and state policy that have not yet been broached with our counterparts among the states and that it will require action by the state legislatures.

5. Professor Zitzewitz urges that an estimate of the value of losses suffered by shareholders ("the magnitude of shareholder dilution") be provided by the SEC when it settles an enforcement case.

On the whole, the Massachusetts Securities Division supports requiring this disclosure, which will provide additional transparency regarding SEC regulatory settlements. I believe that an estimate of shareholder losses would be quite telling, particularly in instances like the securities analyst cases, which affected the portfolio holdings of millions of investors. In that instance, the estimates would provide support for very substantial fines and other strong remedies.

However, this yardstick must be used with caution. Some abuses may create limited dollar damages, but may reflect fundamental breakdowns in the obligations of financial companies to deal fairly with their customers. Such cases are not trivial, and they call for strong sanctions, even if the damages that can be quantified are comparatively small.

RESPONSE TO POST-HEARING QUESTIONS FROM ERIC W. ZITZEWITZ, STANFORD GRADUATE SCHOOL OF BUSINESS, STANFORD, CALIFORNIA

Replies to follow-up questions
Eric Zitzewitz

1. **Your 2002 study estimated that market timing in certain funds resulted in about $5 billion in annual losses to shareholders, and raised the possibility that investment advisers did not always act decisively to control such risks because they were benefiting financially from permitting frequent trading, as turned out to be the case.**

   To what extent was your study made available to the public? For example, did you share your findings and proposed recommendations in public forums such as conferences or panels attended by industry representatives as well as federal regulators?

   I wrote and circulated the first draft of my paper on stale price arbitrage in January 2000,[1] but the features of the paper you mention were all first added in a March 2002 version.[2] The March version of the paper was posted to both my Stanford website and the Social Science Research Network (www.ssrn.com). SSRN sends weekly email summaries of new papers in specific fields; most economists in academia subscribe, as do many in industry and government. SSRN is the probably the most common vehicle for early dissemination of research, especially in financial economics.

   In June 2002, the Stanford media office wrote a summary of my paper, which they published in the *Stanford Business* alumni magazine and released to the press. This generated some immediate press coverage, including stories on CBS Marketwatch, in Investment News, and on Ignites.com. Stories in the online versions of Business Week (December 2002) and Forbes (March 2003) also discussed my paper.

   As a new assistant professor (I started at Stanford in July 2001), I did not receive as many invitations to conferences, especially industry conferences, as I do now. I did however give a version of my paper at a conference organized by the Mutual Fund Education Alliance for the Intermediary Distribution Council in Chicago in September 2002. I also presented my research at a breakfast in New York organized by FT Interactive Data in October 2002.[3]

   I should mention that my paper was one of at least 6 that discussed stale price

[1] The original version was titled "Daily Net Asset Value Predictability and the Associated Trading Profit Opportunity."
[2] I revised the March version based on referees' comments and circulated a new version in October 2002. This version was published in the *Journal of Law, Economics, and Organization* in their October 2003 issue.
[3] As I have mentioned elsewhere, after I circulated the first draft of my paper in 2000, I was contacted by Interactive Data and began helping them build their fair value pricing model for international equity.

arbitrage prior to September 2003. These other papers were mostly written in late 1999 or early 2000 and were published in journals in 2001-2 (see footnote 4 of my testimony for a list). Of these, Greene and Hodges (2002) also estimated shareholder dilution using the same dataset I used but an earlier time period and slightly different methodology, finding dilution rates for 1998-99 that were about half of what I found for 2001.

How responsive was SEC to the concerns that you raised?

Prior to September 2003, I had very limited contact with the SEC. I had heard from other authors that they had met with the SEC to discuss their papers, and so I made no special effort to contact the SEC directly about my stale price arbitrage paper. I did discuss the issue briefly with a junior SEC economist I met at a conference in April 2002.

I also helped Interactive Data draft a series of notes about fair value pricing, some of these notes referred readers to my papers on my website. These notes were circulated throughout the industry, including to regulators.

After I circulated my paper on late trading in September 2003, I was contacted almost immediately by the SEC and discussed the paper in a conference call with a group of SEC economists. I was invited to give a seminar at the SEC in April 2004, and I then met and discussed my research with many of the SEC's economists.

2. **Do you believe market timing and late trading have diminished since September 2003? What are your views on SEC's actions to curb these abuses? Are any other steps necessary?**

   As I mentioned in my testimony (footnote 7), the industry is now making much greater use of fair value pricing, significantly reducing the arbitrage opportunity in international funds. In the sample of funds for which I have access to daily flow data, shareholder dilution due to market timing has fallen from a peak of over one percent of assets per year to below 0.05%. I also no longer find evidence of late trading in the data.[4]

   Despite this progress, there are still some remaining issues. On average, only about 70 percent of the predictability in international fund net asset values (NAVs) is being removed via fair value pricing. Some funds are using fair value less frequently than I would advise. In addition, many funds use relatively simple models to make their fair value adjustments; theoretically, arbitrageurs with better models could earn profits at the expense of these funds.

[4] I should caution that these statements are based on data from funds willing to share their data with TrimTabs (about 10-15 percent of funds by assets). If there are funds with ongoing timing or late trading issues, one would suppose that are unlikely to be the ones who share their data.

More importantly, valuation issues exist outside of international equity. The most important is in bond funds. Certain types of bonds, such as convertible, high-yield, and municipal bonds, trade very infrequently and with very wide bid-ask spreads. This means that fund NAVs do not fully reflect recent market movements, creating a trading opportunity similar to the one in international equity. Ironically, the improvement in the valuation of international equity funds means that bond funds are now among the most arbitrageable. There is some evidence that arbitrage activity in these funds has been increasing recently, although it is still at very low levels. As I mentioned in my testimony, my impression is that the industry is aware of these issues, but is waiting for the guidance on valuation promised by the SEC.

In general, my view is that the SEC has taken a number of positive steps to address both the specific issues of stale pricing and late trading and the contributing issues in fund governance. My research showed that funds with more independent directors were more likely to have taken steps to limit stale price arbitrage; prior research has shown that these funds also have lower expenses.[5] While these correlations do not necessarily imply that mandating independent chairs and more independent directors will lead to better governance, this seems to me like a reasonable expectation, for commonsense as well as theoretical reasons.

As I mentioned in my testimony, my main critique of post-2003 SEC policy is that the direct response to the market timing issue has thus far focused on limiting trading as opposed to improving fund valuation.

3. **Please explain the basis of your estimate that approximately $5 billion was lost annually as a result of market timing abuses.**

When an investor buys shares in an open end mutual fund, he or she is essentially trading with the fund. When the investor buys, new shares are created, and the investor's cash is added to the assets of the fund. Likewise, when shares are redeemed, cash is taken from the funds assets and paid to the redeeming investor. The "price" of a fund's shares is set by calculating the value of its assets and dividing by the number of share outstanding; this is called the net asset value (NAV) per share.

For this system to work, it is crucial that the fund's assets be valued correctly. The problem with current fund valuation methods is that they under-reflect recent market movements. This means that, on a day in which markets have risen, a "market timer" can predict that a fund's NAV will be below the true value of its assets. If timers buy funds on days that they are underpriced and sell when they are overpriced, they will be depositing too little cash into the fund when they buy

[5] Tufano, Peter and Matthew Sevick, "Board Structure And Fee-Setting In The U.S. Mutual Fund Industry," *Journal of Financial Economics*, 1997, v46 (3,Dec), 321-355.

and withdrawing too much when they sell. This is the primary way in which long-term shareholders' returns are reduced and the one I focused on in my calculation.[6]

In order to calculate the dilution of shareholder returns a given day, you simply need to calculate the difference between the actual NAV and the fund's true value and then multiply this by the number of shares purchased that day. To calculate the true value per share of a fund on a given day, I use a fair value pricing model that corrects for stale pricing in the same way that the models used by industry make the correction. Greene and Hodges (2002) use a different approach: they take the next-day NAV of the fund as a proxy. This yields a noisier estimate of shareholder harm in a small sample, but roughly the same result as my method in a larger sample.

For the funds my sample, I calculated the amount of dilution on each day, and divided this figure by the assets of the fund to get the direct effect of arbitrage on the fund's returns. I then averaged these shareholder dilution rates over time to calculate an annualized dilution rate for each fund. In 2001, for the average international equity fund in my sample, I obtained an average annualized dilution rate of 1.14 percent.

My sample included only about 10-15 percent of the industry, so to estimate an industry-wide figure, I needed to make some assumption about dilution rates outside my sample. Although as mentioned above I was worried that funds choosing to share data with TrimTabs would have below average dilution, to be conservative I assumed that my sample was representative of the industry. There were $417 billion in international equity funds in 2001, so a 1.14 percent dilution rate implies annualized losses of $4.3 billion. Adding the figures for other asset classes led to a total figure of $4.9 billion (see Table 4 of my paper). In most media references to my work, this was rounded up to $5 billion.

Since publishing the paper, I have obtained data for 2000-3 from more funds and have now concluded that, counter to my expectation, dilution rates were higher in the TrimTabs sample than outside, at least prior to September 2003. I still do not have data from all funds, and so have not produced a new formal estimate. My best current guess is that dilution during the six-year period of 1998-2003 was between $10 and $15 billion across all asset classes. In terms of improving the public understanding of these issues, it might be valuable to have the SEC, which should have access to data for almost every fund, produce and publicly report a more definitive figure.

---

[6] In addition, market timers may increase administrative costs or induce the fund to do more trading, increasing commissions and other transactions costs. While these costs are easier for those new to the issue to grasp, they are usually much smaller than the dilution I focus on.

4. **Would more resources and staffing help the SEC do a better job?**

This is difficult for me to assess as an outsider. As I mentioned in my testimony, I believe that, since September 2003, the SEC has been doing a good job on these issues. In addition, to the extent that I would criticize their pre-2003 or even their post-2003 stance on these issues, I do not think that a lack of resources was the primary issue. Adding resources as a substitute for reforms that directly address the issues raised in my testimony seems suboptimal.

That said, since 2003 the SEC has significantly broadened the set of issues it wants its staff to monitor, in investment management as well as in other areas. It seems reasonable to expect that doing this well will require more staff and resources. In addition, resources may be necessary to facilitate other reforms; including those that I advocated in my testimony.

It is difficult to overstate how crucial the efficiency and fairness of our financial services and markets is to the growth of the economy. Even including the increases since 2000, the $900 million budget of the SEC is still modest relative to its mission.